# The Best Things About
# Jelly Rolls
## Non-Fattening
## Sugar Free
## No Cholesterol

Yardage is given for using either
'Jelly Roll' strips or fabric yardage.

Basic Instructions for Cutting, Sewing,
Layering, Quilting and Binding are
on pages 24 - 26.

TIPS: As a Guide for Yardage:
Each $1/4$ yard or a 'Fat Quarter' equals 3 strips.
A pre-cut 'Jelly Roll' strip is 2½" x 44".
Cut 'Fat Quarter' yardage strips to 2½" x 22"

**Peach on Earth Blocks**
pages 4 - 5

Winter Houses
pages 6 - 7

Portugal Medallion
pages 8 - 9

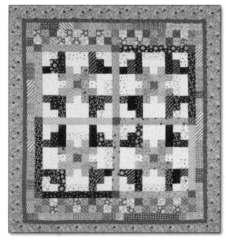

Merry and Bright Poinsettias
page 10

Smores Snowmen and Houses
pages 44 - 45

Fresh Squeezed Tulips
pages 46 - 47

Cranberry Wishes
pages 48 - 49

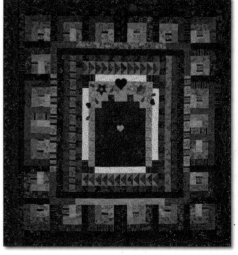

Birchwood Lane House
pages 50 - 51

Cranberry petals burst past the garden gate in three different blocks giving you a variety of complementary possibilities. These comforting colors will blend perfectly with nearly every decor all year long.

Any one of these blocks would make a great accent pillow.

Combine your favorite designs in a small wall hanging or lap quilt.

instructions on pages 31 - 34

# Peace On Earth Blocks

*pieced by Betty Nowlin*
*quilted by Sue Needle*

Peace on Earth
'Jelly Roll'

Winter
'Jelly Roll'

# Winter Houses

*pieced by Betty Nowlin*
*quilted by Sue Needle*

*Create a welcoming community of homes softly frosted with winter's colors. This is a must-do project for everyone who loves house blocks. Enjoy the single-story ranch-style, multi-level modern, and a traditional English manor as well as the neighborhood church. Whether you create a winter wonderland for your home or change the fabrics to suit your favorite seasons, this quilt is destined to become a neighborhood prize.*

instructions on pages 16 - 21

# Portugal Medallion

### pieced by Kayleen Allen
### quilted by Sue Needle

*Masterful color placement makes this Trip Around the World variation an absolute delight to behold. Bright colors keep your eye entertained as it moves around this fabulous design. With strips arranged in columns, this quilt is also a delight to construct.*

instructions on pages 22 - 23

Portugal
'Jelly Roll'

# Merry & Bright Poinsettias

*pieced by Edna Summers*
*quilted by Sue Needle*

Someone's holiday is about to become far merrier and much brighter when they open their present to discover this jolly quilt. Perfect for holiday decorating, this poinsettia treasure is a welcome gift for everyone on your list.

Simple block construction insures that you will have this one done before you can say "Happy Christmas to All and to All a Good Night!"

instructions on pages 11 - 12

Merry & Bright
'Jelly Rolls'

# Merry & Bright Poinsettias

PHOTO ON PAGE 10

SIZE: 56" x 64"

YARDAGE:

We used a *Moda* "Merry and Bright" by Sandy Gervais
'Jelly Roll' collection of 2½" fabric strips
- we purchased 1 'Jelly Roll'

| | | |
|---|---|---|
| ⅔ yard White | OR | 9 strips |
| ⅔ yard Red | OR | 9 strips |
| ½ yard Blue | OR | 6 strips |
| ⅝ yard Green | OR | 8 strips |
| ⅓ yard Gold | OR | 4 strips |
| ¼ yard Plaid | OR | 3 strips |
| ⅓ yard Stripe | OR | 4 strips |

| | |
|---|---|
| Border #2 | Purchase ¼ yard Turquoise |
| Border #3 & Binding | Purchase 1⅝ yards Green |
| Backing | Purchase 3¼ yards |
| Batting | Purchase 64" x 72" |

Sewing machine, needle, thread

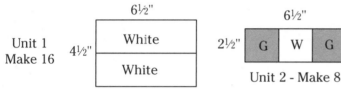

Unit 1
Make 16

Unit 2 - Make 8

SPEED PIECING:

**Unit 1:**
Sew 3 White strips end to end and cut a piece 104" long.
   Set aside the leftovers for cutting small pieces.
Repeat with 3 White strips to make another 104" piece.
Sew the 2 long White strips together side by side to make
   a strip 4½" x 104'.
Cut this piece into 16 units, each 4½" x 6½".

**Unit 2:**
Cut 1 White and 2 Green strips, each 20" long.
Sew the strips together: Green-White-Green
   to make a piece 6½" x 20". Press.
Cut this piece into 8 units, each 2½" x 6½".

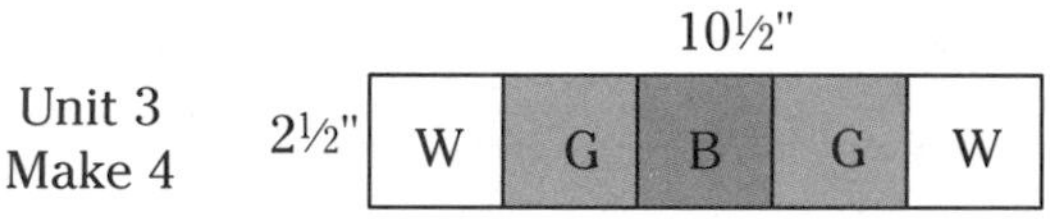

Unit 3
Make 4

**Unit 3:**
Cut 1 Blue, 2 White, 2 Green strips, each 10" long.
Sew the strips together: White-Green-Blue-Green-White
   to make a piece 10' x 10½".
Cut this piece into 4 pieces, each 2½" x 10½".

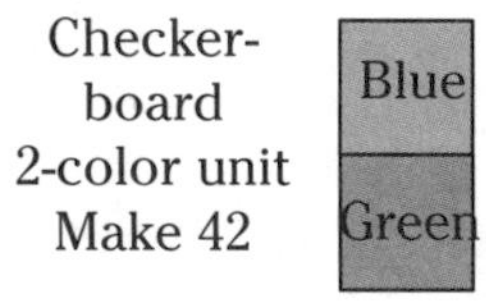

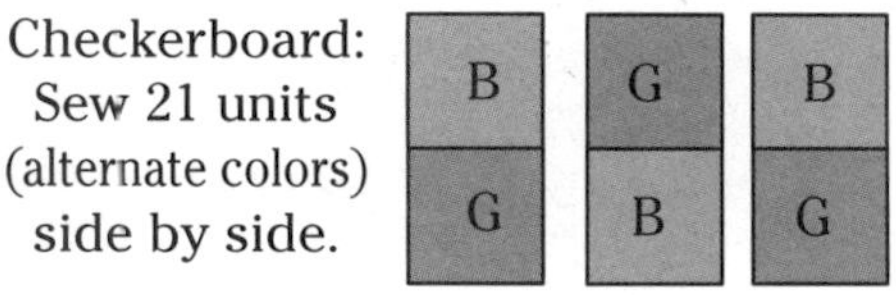

Checker-
board
2-color unit
Make 42

Checkerboard:
Sew 21 units
(alternate colors)
side by side.

**Green-Blue Checkerboard Top and Bottom Border:**
Sew 3 Green strips end to end and cut a piece 106".
Repeat with 3 Blue strips to make another 106" piece.
Sew Green and Blue strips together side by side to make
   4½" x 106".
Cut 42 checkerboard 2-color units, each 2½" x 4½".
Following the diagram, sew 21 units together.
   Press. Make 2.

## CUTTING CHART:

TIP: All strips are 2½" wide by the indicated measurement.

TIP: You may need to sew smaller strips end to end to enable
   you to cut a longer piece. This adds to the charm of the
   scrappy look.

TIP: Label the pieces as you cut.

**White**

| Quantity | Length | Position |
|---|---|---|
| 16 | 4½" | Blocks A and B |
| 16 | 2½" | Blocks A and B |

**Red**

| | | |
|---|---|---|
| 4 | 18½" | Sashing |
| 16 | 6½" | Blocks A and B |
| 16 | 4½" | Blocks A and B |
| 16 | 2½" | Blocks A and B |

**Blue**

| | | |
|---|---|---|
| 9 | 2½" | Sashing cornerstones |

**Green**

| | | |
|---|---|---|
| 8 | 10½" | Block D |

**Gold**

| | | |
|---|---|---|
| 8 | 18½" | Sashing |

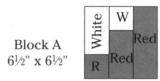

Block A
6½" x 6½"

## PREPARATION FOR BLOCKS

**Block A:**
   Make 8 of each:
   Column 1: Sew a White 4½" strip to a Red 2½" square. Press.
   Column 2: Sew a White 2½" square to a Red 4½" strip. Press.
   Sew Column 1 to Column 2. Press.
   Sew a Red 6½" strip to the right side. Press.

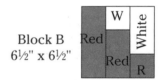

Block B
6½" x 6½"

**Block B:**
   Make 8 of each:
   Column 1: Sew a White 2½" square to a Red 4½" strip. Press.
   Column 2: Sew a White 4½" strip to a Red 2½" square. Press.
   Sew Column 1 to Column 2. Press.
   Sew a Red 6½" strip to the left side. Press.

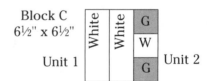

Block C
6½" x 6½"

Unit 1        Unit 2

**Block C:**
   Make 8.
   Sew a Unit 2 to the bottom of a Unit 1. Press.

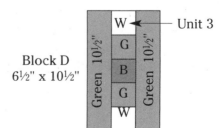

Block D
6½" x 10½"

**Block D:**
   Make 4.
   Sew a Green 10½" strip to each long side of a Unit 3.
   Press.

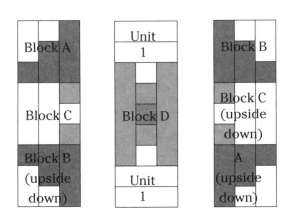

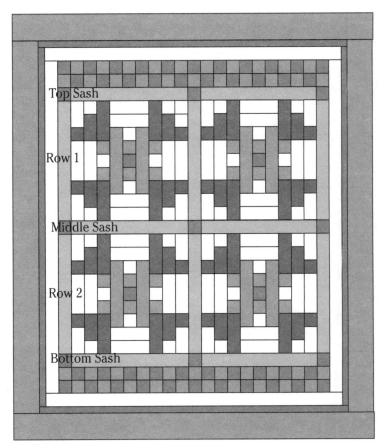

## SEW BIG BLOCKS:

Make 4. Refer to the Block Assembly diagram for color placement and position.

**Column 1:** Sew Block A - Block C - Block B. Press.

**Column 2:** Sew Unit 1 - Block D - Unit 1. Press.

**Column 3:** Sew Block B - Block C (upside down) - Block A (upside down). Press.

**Sew the columns together.**

Press. Each Poinsettia Block will measure 18½" x 18½" at this point.

Poinsettia Block - Make 4

Merry & Bright Poinsettias - Quilt Assembly

## SASHING:

You'll need 4 Gold 18½" strips, 2 Red 18½" strips and 9 Blue 2½" squares.

Sew the following in a row:

**Top Sash:**
Blue - Gold 18½" - Blue - Red 18½" - Blue.

**Middle Sash:**
Blue - Gold 18½" - Blue - Gold 18½" - Blue.

**Bottom Sash:**
Blue - Red 18½" - Blue - Gold 18½" - Blue.

## ASSEMBLY:

Arrange all Blocks on a work surface or table.
Refer to diagram for block placement and direction.
You'll need 4 Gold 18½" strips, 2 Red 18½" strips and 4 Big Blocks.

**Row 1:**
Sew a Gold - Block - Gold - Block - Red. Press.
Sew the Top sash to the top of Row 1. Press.
Sew the Middle sash to the bottom of Row 1. Press.

**Row 2:**
Sew a Red - Block - Gold - Block - Gold. Press.
Sew Row 2 to the bottom of the piece. Press.
Sew the Bottom sash to the bottom of the piece. Press.

**Checkerboard Borders - Top and Bottom:**
Sew a Checkerboard to the top of the quilt.
Press.
Sew a Checkerboard to the bottom of the quilt.
Press.

## BORDERS:

**Scrappy Pieced Borders:**
Randomly cut leftover strips into 4" and 8" strips. Sew them together end to end.
Cut 2 strips 50½" for sides.
Cut 2 strips 46½" for top and bottom.
Sew side borders to the quilt. Press.
Sew top and bottom borders to the quilt. Press.

**Border #2:**
Cut five strips 1½" x width of fabric.
Sew strips together end to end.
Cut 2 strips 1½" x 54½" for sides.
Cut 2 strips 1½" x 48½" for top and bottom.
Sew side borders to the quilt. Press.
Sew top and bottom borders to the quilt. Press.

**Border #3:**
Cut the strips parallel to the selvage to eliminate piecing.
Cut 2 strips 4½" x 56½" for sides.
Cut 2 strips 4½" x 56½" for top and bottom.
Sew side borders to the quilt. Press.
Sew top and bottom borders to the quilt. Press.

## FINISHING:

**Quilting**:
See Basic Instructions on pages 24 - 26.

**Binding**:
Cut strips 2½" wide.
Sew together end to end to equal 250".
See Binding Instructions on page 26.

# Smores Snowmen and Houses

PHOTO ON PAGES 44 - 45

SIZE: 52" x 60"

YARDAGE:

We used a *Moda* "Smores" by Me & My Sister 'Jelly Roll' collection of 2½" fabric strips - we purchased 1 'Jelly Roll'

| ½ yard Turquoise | OR | 6 strips |
| ⅛ yard Tan | OR | 1 strip |
| ½ yard Green | OR | 6 strips |
| ½ yard White print | OR | 6 strips |
| ½ yard Pink | OR | 6 strips |
| ⅜ yard Purple | OR | 5 strips |

| Solid White Snowmen | Purchase ⅜ yard Solid White |
| Border #4 | Purchase ¼ yard Turquoise print |
| Border #5 & Binding | Purchase 1½ yards Pink print |
| Backing | Purchase 3 yards |
| Batting | Purchase 60" x 68" |
| Buttons | 6 - ⅝" for eyes, 9 ⅝" for shirt |
| Beads | 27 - 3 x 6mm Black beads for mouth |
| Sewing machine, needle. thread | |

CUTTING:

Tip: All strips are 2½" wide by the indicated measurements. Cut the longest strips first.

Tip: You may need to sew smaller strips end to end to enable you to cut a longer piece. This adds to the charm of the scrappy look.

## White Print

Set aside 3 White print strips for the pieced border.
You need 3 White print strips for the Houses.
(1 with Green print, 1 with Purple print, 1 with Pink print)

| Quantity | Length | Position |
|---|---|---|
| 3 | 10½" | Houses A, B & C above door for top row |
| | | (1 with Green print, 1 with Purple print, 1 with Pink print) |
| 12 | 8½" | House A, B & C for sides |
| | | (4 with Green print, 4 with Purple print, 4 with Pink print) |

## Solid White

| 27 | 6½" | Head, middle, and base for all Snowmen |

## Turquoise

You need 3 strips.
Set aside 3 strips for the pieced border.

| Quantity | Length | Position |
|---|---|---|
| 6 | 10½" | 5 for snowman A, 1 for roof C |
| 3 | 6½" | 2 for snowman A 1 for roof C |
| 2 | 2½" | 2 for house B sky |
| 12 | 2½" | for snowman A corner squares |

## Green

You need 3 strips.
Set aside 3 strips for the pieced border.

| 7 | 10½" | 5 for snowman B 1 for roof A 1 for roof B |
| 3 | 6½" | 2 for snowman B, 1 for roof B |
| 4 | 2½" | 2 for houses A sky 2 for house C sky |
| 12 | 2½" | for snowman B corner squares |

## Pink

You need 3 strips.
Set aside 3 strips for the pieced border.

| 5 | 10½" | 4 for snowman C, 1 for roof A |
| 3 | 6½" | 2 for snowman C 1 for roof A |
| 12 | 2½" | for snowman C corner squares |

## Tan

You need 1 strip.

| 3 | 8½" | for houses A, B & C doors |
| 6 | 2½" | for snowmen A, B & C arms |

---

PREPARATION FOR BLOCKS

### Snowman Blocks:

Note: Sew all snowmen in the same sequence. The only difference between the snowmen is the surrounding color.
> Snowman A is surrounded by Turquoise.
> Snowman B is surrounded by Green.
> Snowman C is surrounded by Pink.

### 'Snowballs' for Heads & Bodies:

> Sew 3 Solid White 6½" strips together side by side to make a 6½" square. Press.
> Make 9 'Snowball' squares.

### Snowball Corners:

> Refer to the Snowball Corners diagram.
> Align a 2½" square of the surrounding color in the corner.
> Draw a diagonal as shown. Sew on the line and fold the corner back. Press. Trim excess fabric from underneath.
> Make 9.

### Heads:

> Strip color is determined by the surrounding color of the corners.
> **Side Borders:** Sew a 6½" strip to each side of the head. Press.
> **Top Border:** Sew a 10½" strip to the top of the head.
> Make 3.

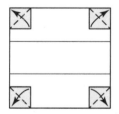

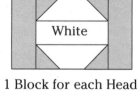
Surrounding Color
White
1 Block for each Head

Snowman Corner Diagram

2 Blocks for each Body

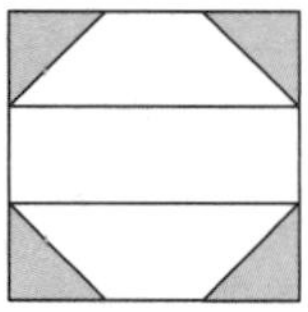

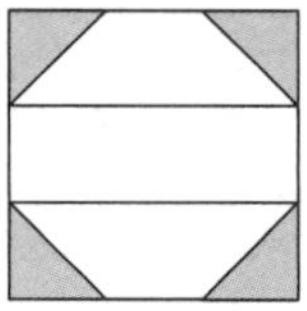

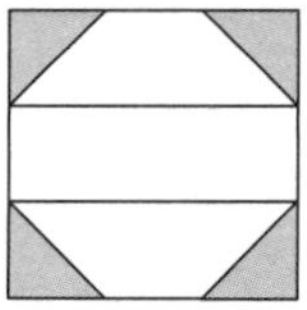

**Bodies:**

Sew the snowball middle shirt body to the base body. Press.

**Side Strips:** Sew a Tan 2½"arm square to a 10½" surrounding color strip for each side of block. Press. Make 2 of each surrounding color.

Sew a side strips to each side of the body. Press.

**Assemble Snowmen:**

Sew the head section to the body section. Press.

Sew a surrounding color 10½" strip to the bottom of snowmen A, B and C.

Sew an additional surrounding color 10½" strip to the top of snowman A and snowman B.

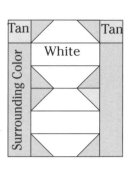

Snowman Body
Make 3

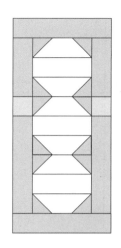

Snowman C

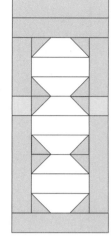

Snowmen
A and B

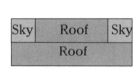

Roof Section for
B & C

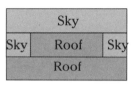

Roof Section
for A

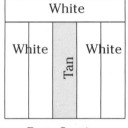

Base Section

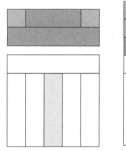

House Blocks
B & C

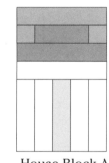

House Block A

**Houses A, B and C:**

**House Roof & Sky Sections:**

Sew the following:

**House A:** Green 2½" square - Pink 6½" strip - Green square. Sew this and a Pink 10½" strip together side by side. Sew a Green 10½" strip to the top of House A. Press.

**House B:** Turquoise 2½" square - Green 6½" strip - Turquoise square. Sew this and a Green 10½" strip together side by side.

**House C:** Green 2½" square - Turquoise 6½" strip - Green square. Sew this and a Turquoise 10½" strip together side by side.

**House Base Sections:**

Sew five 8½" strips together side by side: 2 White print - 1 Tan print - 2 White print to make a piece 8½" x 10½". Press.

Turn the piece so the seams are vertical. Sew a White print 10½" strip to the top of the block. Press.

**House Block:**

Sew the base section to the roof section. Press.

**Column Assembly:**

**Column 1:** Sew house B to bottom of snowman A. Press.

**Column 2:** Sew snowman C to bottom of house A. Press.

**Column 3:** Sew house C to bottom of snowman B. Press.

Each block will measure 10½" x 38½" at this point.

ASSEMBLY:

Arrange all Blocks on a work surface or table. Refer to diagram for block placement and direction. Sew columns 1-2-3 together. Press.

BORDERS:

**Purple-White Checkerboard Border #1:**

You need 2 strips plus 6" of Purple. Sew the 3 Purple strips together end to end.

You need 2 strips plus 6" of White print. Sew the 3 White strips together end to end.

Sew the long Purple strip and the long White strip together side by side to make a piece 4½" wide. Press.

Cut the strips into 34 units 2½" x 4½". Cut 2 White and 2 Purple 2½" squares.

**Side Checkerboard Borders:**

For each side, sew 1 White square and 9 Purple-White units to make a strip 38½" long. Press. Sew the side borders to the quilt. Press.

**Top and Bottom Checkerboard Borders:**

For each border, sew 8 Purple-White units and 1 Purple square to make a strip 34½" long. Sew the top and bottom borders to the quilt. Press.

## Purple-Turquoise Checkerboard Border #2:

You need 3 Purple and 3 Turquoise strips.

Sew a Purple and Turquoise strip together side by side to make a piece 4½" wide. Press.

Make 3.

Cut the Purple-Turquoise strips into 33 units 2½" x 4½".

Cut 2 Turquoise and 2 Purple 2½" squares and set them aside.

### Side Borders:

For each side, sew 10 Turquoise-Purple units and 1 Turquoise square to make a strip 42½" long. Press.

Sew the side borders to the quilt. Press.

### Top and Bottom Borders:

For each border, sew 9 Purple-Turquoise units and 1 Purple square to make a strip 38½" long.

Sew the top and bottom borders to the quilt. Press.

## Green-Pink Checkerboard Border #3:

You need 3 Pink and 3 Green strips.

Sew a Pink and Green strip together side by side to make a piece 4½" wide. Press.

Make 3.

Cut strips into 42 units 2½" x 4½".

Cut 2 Pink and 2 Green 2½" squares.

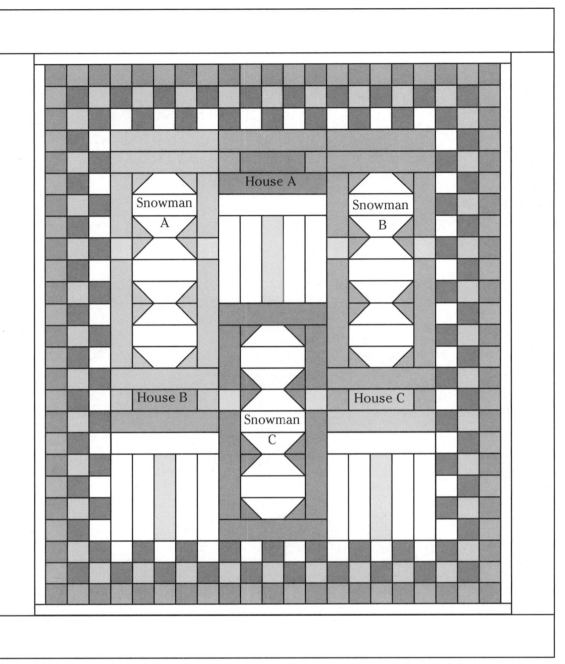

Smores Snowmen and Houses - Quilt Assembly

Snowmen Face and Shirt Body

### Side Borders:

For each side, sew 11 Green-Pink units and 1 Green square to make a strip 46½" long. Press.

Sew the side borders to the quilt. Press.

### Top and Bottom Borders:

For each border, sew 10 Pink-Green units and 1 Pink square to make a strip 42½" long.

Sew the top and bottom borders to the quilt. Press.

### Border #4:

Cut 5 strips 1½" x 42" by the width of fabric. Sew strips together end to end.

Cut 2 strips 1½" x 50½" for sides.

Cut 2 strips 1½" x 44½" for top and bottom.

Sew side borders to the quilt. Press.

Sew top and bottom borders to the quilt. Press.

### Border #5:

Cut the strips parallel to the selvage to eliminate piecing on the long borders.

Cut 2 strips 4½" x 52½" for sides.

Cut 2 strips 4½" x 52½" for top and bottom.

Sew side borders to the quilt. Press.

Sew top and bottom borders to the quilt. Press.

### FINISHING:

**Quilting**:

See Basic Instructions on pages 24 - 26.

**Binding**:

Cut strips 2½" wide.

Sew together end to end to equal 234".

See Binding Instructions on page 26.

BUTTONS: Sew buttons and beads on snowmen. DO NOT use buttons or beads on baby/toddler or young children quilts.

# Winter Houses

PHOTO ON PAGES 6 - 7

SIZE: 56" x 64"

YARDAGE:
We used a *Moda* "Winter" by Minicks & Simpson
'Jelly Roll' collection of 2½" fabric strips
- we purchased 1 'Jelly Roll'

| ⅞ yard White | OR | 12 strips |
|---|---|---|
| ⅔ yard Green | OR | 9 strips |
| ⅝ yard Red | OR | 8 strips |
| ½ yard Blue | OR | 7 strips |
| ¼ yard Stripe or Light | OR | 3 strips |

| Border #3 | Purchase ¼ yard Red |
|---|---|
| Border #4 & Binding | Purchase 1⅝ yards White print |
| Backing | Purchase 3¼ yards |
| Batting | Purchase 64" x 72" |

Sewing machine, needle, thread

Tip: When possible, cut the longest pieces first.

SPEED PIECING:

**Unit 1:**
Cut 1 Blue and 1 Red strip 17½" long.
Sew the strips together side by side to make a piece 4½" x 17½". Press.
Cut this piece into 7 units 2½" x 4½"
    (2 for House B, 4 for House C, 1 for Church).

**Unit 2:**
Cut 1 Blue and 1 Green strip 5" long.
Sew the strips together side by side to make a piece 4½" x 5". Press.
Cut this piece into 2 units 2½" x 4½" (2 for House A).

**Unit 3:**
Cut 1 White and 1 Red strip 5" long.
Sew the strips together side by side to make a piece 4½" x 5". Press.
Cut this piece into 2 units 2½" x 4½" (2 for House B).

SASHING:
Randomly cut 6 Green strips into sections and sew them end to end.

Cut 3 Green strips 38½" long for the top, middle and bottom sashing.
Save the leftover for the Green pieced border.

Cut 2 White strips 38½" long for the top and middle sashing.
Sew a White sash to a Green sash to make a piece 4½" x 38½".
Make 2. Press.
The remaining Green sash goes on the bottom.

**For Side Sashings:**
Cut 3 White strips 22½" long and 3 White strips 18½" long.

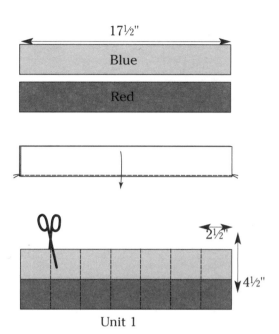

Unit 1

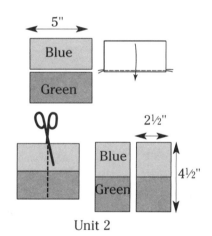

Unit 2

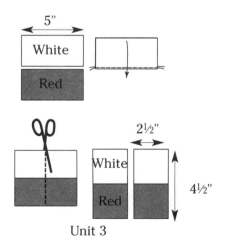

Unit 3

## CUTTING CHART:

TIP: All strips are 2½" wide by the indicated measurement.
Label the pieces as you cut and group the pieces by building.

TIP: You may need to sew smaller strips end to end to enable you to
cut a longer piece. This adds to the charm of the scrappy look.

**White**

| Quantity | Length | Position |
|---|---|---|
| 1 | 18½" | House A #21 |
| 1 | 16½" | House C #22 |
| 4 | 10½" | House A #19, 20, Church #14, 15 |
| 2 | 8½" | Church #9, 13 |
| 6 | 6½" | House A #17, House B #14, House C #18, 19, 21, Church #7 |
| 3 | 4½" | House C #11, Church #25, 26 |
| 6 | 2½" | House A #15, House C #7, 12, 16, Church #19, 23 |

**Green**

| Quantity | Length | Position |
|---|---|---|
| 2 | 14½" | Church #8, 20 |
| 1 | 10½" | House C #8 |
| 7 | 8½" | House A #9,10, House C #6, 10, 17, Church #11, 21 |
| 3 | 4½" | House A #6, 8, Church #17 |
| 1 | 2½" | House A #16 |

**Red**

| Quantity | Length | Position |
|---|---|---|
| 3 | 14½" | House B #15, House C #9, 13 |
| 2 | 10½" | House A #4, 18 |
| 9 | 8½" | House A #11, 12, 13, 14, House B #13, House C #14, Church #10, 18, 22 |
| 5 | 6½" | House B #6, 11, Church #4, 5, 6 |
| 4 | 4½" | House A #5, 7, House B #4, 9 |

**Blue**

| Quantity | Length | Position |
|---|---|---|
| 2 | 12½" | House B #5, 10 |
| 8 | 10½" | House A #2, 3, House B #3, 8, House C #3, 4, 5, Church #16 |
| 1 | 8½" | House C #15 |
| 5 | 6½" | House B #2, 7, 12, Church #2, 3 |
| 1 | 4½" | House C #20 |
| 6 | 2½" | House A #1, House C #1, 2, Church #1, 12, 24 |

## PREPARATION FOR BLOCKS

## House A:

**Window Section:**
Sew 2 Blue-Green Unit 2's and a Blue #1 in a line to make a
strip 2½" x 10½". Press.
Sew Blue #2 and Blue #3 above and below the strip. Press.
Sew Red #4 to the top of the piece. Press.

**Door Section:**
Sew Red #5 to Green #6. Press.
Sew Red #7 to Green #8. Press.
Sew the pieces together, matching the Reds and Greens. Press.
Sew Green #9 and 10 on the sides of the piece.
Sew the Window and Door sections together. Press.

**Chimney Section:**
Sew White #15 - Green #16 - White #17. Press.
Sew Red #18 to the bottom of the piece. Press.
Sew White #19 and 20 to the top of the piece. Press.

**Roof Section:**
Sew Red strips #11-12-13-14 to make a piece 8½" x 8½". Press.
Sew the Roof section to the Chimney section. Press.
Sew the White sky #21 to the top of the Chimney-Roof. Press.
Sew the Chimney-Roof section to the Window-Door section. Press.

**House A**

| 21 | Sky |
|---|---|

| 20 | |
|---|---|
| Chimney | 19 |
| 15 | 16 | 17 |
| 18 | |

| | 14 |
|---|---|
| Roof | 13 |
| | 12 |
| | 11 |

| 4 |
|---|
| 3 |
| Unit 2 | Unit 2 | 1 |
| 2 |

Window

| 9 | 6 | 8 | 10 |
|---|---|---|---|
| | 5 | 7 | |

Door

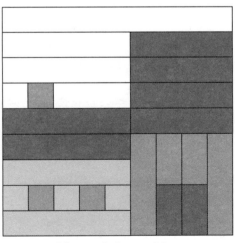

House A Assembly

**House B**

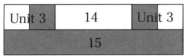

Unit 3 | 14 | Unit 3

15

Section C

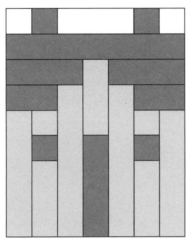

Section A  Door  Section B

House B Assembly

**House C**

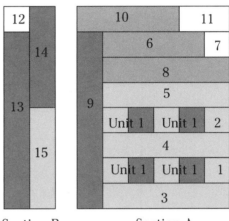

22

19 | 20 | 21

16 | 17 | 18

Section C

Section B  Section A

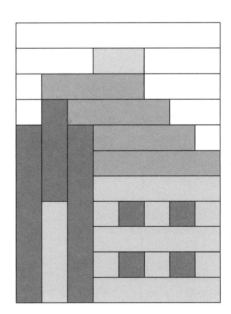

House C Assembly

# House B:

**Section A:**
Sew a Blue-Red Unit 1 to Blue #2. Press.
Sew Blue #3 to the left side of the strip. Press.
Sew Red #4 to the top of the piece. Press.
Sew Blue #5 to the right side of the piece. Press.
Sew Red #6 to the top of the piece. Press.

**Section B:**
Sew a Blue-Red Unit 1 to Blue #7. Press.
Sew Blue #8 to the right side of the strip. Press.
Sew Red #9 to the top of the piece. Press.
Sew Blue #10 to the left side of the piece. Press.
Sew Red #11 to the top of the piece.
Sew Blue #12 and Red #13 end to end to make the
    door strip. Press.
Sew the door strip to the left side of section B. Press.
Sew section A to section B. Press.

**Section C:**
Sew a White-Red Unit 3 to each end of White #14. Press.
Sew Red #15 to the bottom of the piece. Press.
Sew the Chimney section to the A-B section. Press.

## House C:
### Section A:
Sew 2 Blue-Red Unit 1's and a Blue #1 to make a strip 10½" long. Press.

Sew 2 Blue-Red Unit 1's and a Blue #2 to make a strip 10½" long. Press.

Sew Blue #3 to the bottom of one strip piece.

Sew Blue #4 to the top of the same strip. Press.

Sew the second unit section to the top of the piece. Press.

Sew Blue #5 to the top of a unit section. Press.

Sew Green #6 to White #7. Press.

Sew Green #8 to the bottom of the Green-White piece. Press.

Sew this to the top of section A. Press.

Sew Red #9 to the left side of section A. Press.

Sew Green #10 and White #11 end to end. Press.

Sew 10-11 to the top of section A. Press.

### Section B:
Sew White #12 and Red #13 end to end. Press.

Sew Red #14 to Blue #15 end to end. Press.

Sew 12-13 to 14-15. Press.

Sew section A to section B. Press.

### Section C:
Sew White #16 - Green #17 - White #18 end to end. Press.

Sew White #19 - Blue #20 - White #21 end to end. Press.

Sew strip 16-17-18 to strip 19-20-21. Press.

Sew White strip #22 to the top of the piece. Press.

Sew section C to the top of section A-B. Press.

## Church

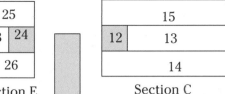

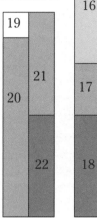

Section E

Section C

Section D

Section A

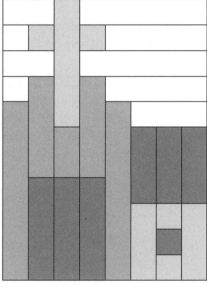

Church Assembly

## Church:
### Section A:
Sew a Blue-Red Unit 1 to Blue #1. Press.

Sew Blue #2 and #3 to the unit section. Press.

### Section B:
Sew Red strips #4-5-6 together. Press.

Sew White #7 to the top of the piece. Press.

Sew Section A to Section B. Press.

Sew Green #8 to the left side. Press.

Sew White #9 to the top. Press.

Sew Red #10 to Green #11 end to end. Press.

Sew the 10-11 strip to the left side of section A-B. Press.

### Section C:
Sew Blue #12 to White #13. Press.

Sew White #14 and 15 to the top and bottom of the strip. Press.

Sew section C to the top of section A-B. Press.

Sew Blue #16 - Green #17 - Red #18 end to end. Press.

Sew this strip to the left side of section A-B-C. Press.

### Section D:
Sew White #19 to Green #20. Press.

Sew Green #21 to Red #22. Press.

Sew the strips together. Press.

### Section E:
Sew White #23 to Blue #24. Press.

Sew White #25 and 26 to the top and bottom of the strip. Press.

Sew sections D and E together. Press.

Sew D-E to A-B-C. Press.

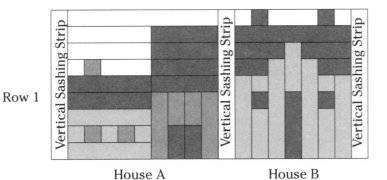

Row 1

House A      House B

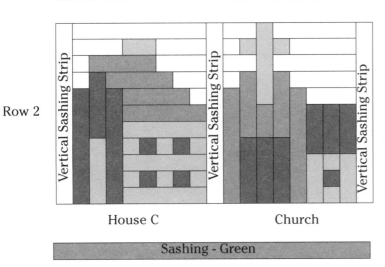

Row 2

House C      Church

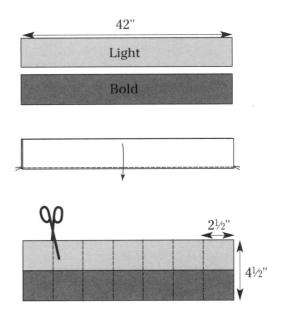

## ASSEMBLY:

Arrange all Blocks and sashing strips on a work surface or table.

The 18½" vertical sashing strips are on Row 1.

The 22½" vertical sashing strips are on Row 2.

Refer to diagram for block placement and direction.

**Row 1:**

Sew Sash - House A - Sash - House B - Sash. Press.

Sew the Top Green-White horizontal sash to the top of Row 1. Press.

Sew the Middle Green-White horizontal sash to the bottom of Row 1. Press.

**Row 2:**

Sew Sash - House C - Sash - Church - Sash. Press.

Sew Row 2 to the bottom of the piece. Press.

Sew Green horizontal sash to the bottom of the piece. Press.

## Prepare Checkerboard Border:

Choose 3 leftover bold strips for the mix (2 Blue and 1 Red) and 3 lighter strips.

Sew a bold and light together side by side to make a piece 4½" x 42".

Make 3. Press.

Cut 46 units 2½" x 4½".

In addition, cut 2 bold and 2 light 2½" squares.

**Side Borders: Make 2.**

Sew 12 units together, Red bold-light, Blue bold-light, etc.

Sew a light square on one end to make a piece 50½" long. Press.

## Top and Bottom Borders: Make 2.

Sew 11 units together, light-Red bold, light-Blue bold, etc.

Sew a bold square on one end to make a piece 46½" long. Press.

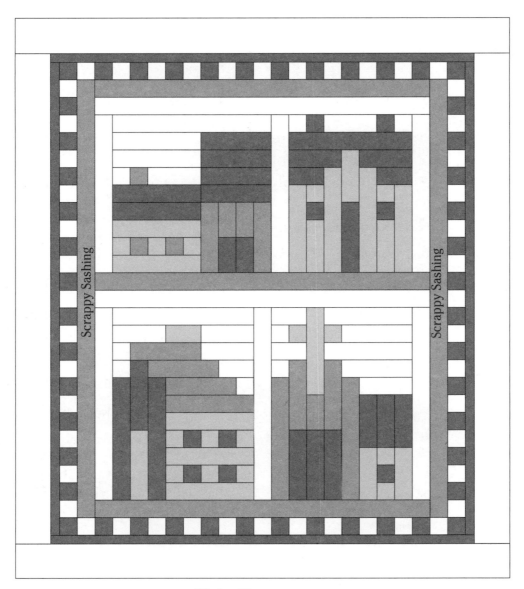

Winter Houses
Quilt Assembly

**Scrappy Pieced Side Border:**
Using the Green scrappy strip from the sashings,
  cut 2 strips 50½" long for the sides.
Sew side borders to the quilt. Press.
The quilt should measure 42½" x 50½" at this point.

BORDERS:
**Checkerboard Border:**
Sew side checkerboard border strips to the quilt. Press.
Sew the top and bottom checkerboard borders. Press.

**Border #3:**
Cut 5 strips 1½" x width of fabric.
Sew strips together end to end.
  Cut 2 strips 1½" x 54½" for sides.
  Cut 2 strips 1½" x 48½" for top and bottom.
  Sew side borders to the quilt. Press.
  Sew top and bottom borders to the quilt. Press.

**Border #4:**
Cut the strips parallel to the selvage to eliminate piecing on the long borders.
  Cut 2 strips 4½" x 56½" for sides.
  Cut 2 strips 4½" x 56½" for top and bottom.
  Sew side borders to the quilt. Press.
  Sew top and bottom borders to the quilt. Press.

FINISHING:
**Quilting**:
  See Basic Instructions on pages 24 - 26.
**Binding**:
  Cut strips 2½" wide.
  Sew together end to end to equal 250".
  See Binding Instructions on page 26.

# Portugal Medallion

PHOTO ON PAGES 8 - 9

SIZE: 56" x 68"

YARDAGE:
We used a *Moda* "Portugal" by April Cornell
'Jelly Roll' collection of 2½" fabric strips
- we purchased 1 'Jelly Roll'

| | | |
|---|---|---|
| ½ yard Yellow | OR | 7 strips |
| ½ yard Blue | OR | 7 strips |
| ½ yard Red | OR | 6 strips |
| ⅔ yard Gold | OR | 9 strips |
| ¼ yard Green | OR | 3 strips |

| | |
|---|---|
| Border #1 | Purchase ¼ yard Red |
| Border #2 & Binding | Purchase 1⅝ yards Blue print |
| Backing | Purchase 3⅓ yards |
| Batting | Purchase 64" x 76" |

Sewing machine, needle, thread

PREPARATION FOR QUILT DESIGN:
Organize your fabric strips
Caution:
> Cut carefully.
> Cut the longest strips first.

CUTTING CHART:
TIP: All strips are 2½" wide by the indicated measurement.
TIP: You may need to sew smaller strips end to end to enable you to cut a longer piece. This adds to the charm of the scrappy look.
TIP: Label the pieces as you cut.

**Yellow**
You'll need 7 strips.

| Quantity | Length | Position |
|---|---|---|
| 1 | 10½" | Center |
| 2 | 6½" | Center |
| 32 | 6½" | Medallion 5 |
| 4 | 4½" | Medallion 5 |
| 4 | 2½" | Medallion 5 |
| 2 | 2½" | Center |

**Blue**
You'll need 7 strips.

| Quantity | Length | Medallion # |
|---|---|---|
| 2 | 14½" | 1 |
| 2 | 10½" | 1 |
| 4 | 10½" | 7 |
| 10 | 8½" | 1 |
| 4 | 8½" | 7 |
| 2 | 6½" | 1 |
| 4 | 6½" | 7 |
| 4 | 4½" | 7 |
| 4 | 2½" | 7 |
| 2 | 2½" | 1 |

**Red**
You'll need 6 strips.

| Quantity | Length | Medallion # |
|---|---|---|
| 2 | 6½" | 2 |
| 26 | 4½" | 2 |
| 24 | 4½" | 6 |
| 4 | 2½" | 6 |
| 2 | 2½" | 2 |

**Gold**
You'll need 9 strips.

| Quantity | Length | Medallion # |
|---|---|---|
| 2 | 14½" | 3 |
| 2 | 10½" | 3 |
| 34 | 8½" | 3 |

**Green**
You'll need 3 strips.

| Quantity | Length | Medallion # |
|---|---|---|
| 42 | 2½" | 4 |

ASSEMBLY:
Arrange all cut strips and squares according to the quilt assembly diagram.
Note the color and strip size placement.
Mark the pieces for each column with the number that appears in the diagram.
Sew pieces together in each column from top to bottom. Press.
Sew the columns together. Press.

BORDERS:
**Border #1:**
Cut 5 strips 1½" x width of fabric.
Sew strips together end to end.
> Cut 2 strips 1½" x 54½" for sides.
> Cut 2 strips 1½" x 44½" for top and bottom.
> Sew side borders to the quilt. Press.
> Sew top and bottom borders to the quilt. Press.

**Border #2:**
Cut the strips parallel to the selvage to eliminate piecing on the long borders.
> Cut 2 strips 6½" x 56½" for sides.
> Cut 2 strips 6½" x 56½" for top and bottom.
> Sew side borders to the quilt. Press.
> Sew top and bottom borders to the quilt. Press.

FINISHING:
**Quilting:**
> See Basic Instructions on pages 24 - 26.
**Binding:**
> Cut strips 2½" wide.
> Sew together end to end to equal 258".
> See Binding Instructions on page 26.

Portugal Medallion
Quilt Assembly

# Tips for Working with Strips

**TIPS:  As a Guide for Yardage:**
Each ¼ yard or a 'Fat Quarter' equals 3 strips
A pre-cut 'Jelly Roll' strip is 2½" x 44"
Cut 'Fat Quarter' strips to 2½" x 22"

Pre-cut strips are cut on the crosswise grain and are prone to stretching. These tips will help reduce stretching and make your quilt lay flat for quilting.

1. If you are cutting yardage, cut on the grain. Cut fat quarters on grain, parallel to the 18" side.

2. When sewing crosswise grain strips together, take care not to stretch the strips. If you detect any puckering as you go, rip out the seam and sew it again.

3. Press, Do Not Iron.  Carefully open fabric, with the seam to one side, press without moving the iron. A back-and-forth ironing motion stretches the fabric.

4. Reduce the wiggle in your borders with this technique from garment making. First, accurately cut your borders to the exact measure of the quilt top. Then, before sewing the border to the quilt, run a double row of stay stitches along the outside edge to maintain the original shape and prevent stretching. Pin the border to the quilt, taking care not to stretch the quilt top to make it fit. Pinning reduces slipping and stretching.

## Rotary Cutting Tips

**Rotary Cutter: Friend or Foe**

A rotary cutter is wonderful and useful. When not used correctly, the sharp blade can be a dangerous tool. Follow these safety tips:

1. Never cut toward you.
2. Use a sharp blade. Pressing harder on a dull blade can cause the blade to jump the ruler and injure your fingers.
3. Always disengage the blade before the cutter leaves your hand, even if you intend to pick it up immediately.

Rotary cutters have been caught when lifting fabric, have fallen onto the floor and have cut fingers.

## Basic Sewing Instructions

You now have precisely cut strips that are exactly the correct width. You are well on your way to blocks that fit together perfectly. Accurate sewing is the next important step.

**Matching Edges:**

1. Carefully line up the edges of your strips. Many times, if the underside is off a little, your seam will be off by ⅛". This does not sound like much until you have 8 seams in a block, each off by ⅛". Now your finished block is a whole inch wrong!

2. Pin the pieces together to prevent them shifting.

**Seam Allowance:**

I cannot stress enough the importance of accurate ¼" seams. All the quilts in this book are measured for ¼" seams unless otherwise indicated.

Most sewing machine manufacturers offer a Quarter-inch foot. A Quarter-inch foot is the most worthwhile investment you can make in your quilting.

**Pressing**:

I want to talk about pressing even before we get to

sewing because proper pressing can make the difference between a quilt that wins a ribbon at the quilt show and one that does not.

Press, do NOT iron. What does that mean? Many of us want to move the iron back and forth along the seam. This "ironing" stretches the strip out of shape and creates errors that accumulate as the quilt is constructed. Believe it or not, there is a correct way to press your seams, and here it is:

1. Do NOT use steam with your iron. If you need a little water, spritz it on.

2. Place your fabric flat on the ironing board without opening the seam. Set a hot iron on the seam and count to 3. Lift the iron and move to the next position along the seam. Repeat until the entire seam is pressed. This sets and sinks the threads into the fabric.

3. Now, carefully lift the top strip and fold it away from you so the seam is on one side. Usually the seam is pressed toward the darker fabric, but often the direction of the seam is determined by the piecing requirements.

4. Press the seam open with your fingers. Add a little water or spray starch if it wants to close again. Lift the iron and place it on the seam. Count to 3. Lift the iron again and continue until the seam is pressed. Do NOT use the tip of the iron to push the seam open. So many people do this and wonder later why their blocks are not fitting together.

5. Most critical of all: For accuracy every seam must be pressed before the next seam is sewn.

**Working with 'Crosswise Grain' strips:**

Strips cut on the crosswise grain (from selvage to selvage) have problems similar to bias edges and are prone to stretching. To reduce stretching and make your quilt lay flat for quilting, keep these tips in mind.

1. Take care not to stretch the strips as you sew.

2. Adjust the sewing thread tension and the presser foot pressure if needed.

3. If you detect any puckering as you go, rip out the seam and sew it again. It is much easier to take out a seam now than to do it after the block is sewn.

## Sewing Bias Edges:

Bias edges wiggle and stretch out of shape very easily. They are not recommended for beginners, but even a novice can accomplish bias edges if these techniques are employed.

1. Stabilize the bias edge with one of these methods:

    a) Press with spray starch.

    b) Press freezer paper or removable iron-on stabilizer to the back of the fabric.

    c) Sew a double row of stay stitches along the bias edge and ⅛" from the bias edge. This is a favorite technique of garment makers.

2. Pin, pin, pin! I know many of us dislike pinning, but when working with bias edges, pinning makes the difference between intersections that match and those that do not.

## Building Better Borders:

Wiggly borders make a quilt very difficult to finish. However, wiggly borders can be avoided with these techniques.

1. Cut the borders on grain. That means cutting your strips parallel to the selvage edge.

2. Accurately cut your borders to the exact measure of the quilt.

3. If your borders are piece stripped from crosswise grain fabrics, press well with spray starch and sew a double row of stay stitches along the outside edge to maintain the original shape and prevent stretching.

4. Pin the border to the quilt, taking care not to stretch the quilt top to make it fit. Pinning reduces slipping and stretching.

---

**Embroidery** Use 24" lengths of doubled pearl cotton or 6-ply floss and a #22 or #24 Chenille needle (this needle has a large eye). Outline large elements.

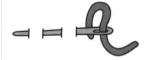 *Running Stitch* Come up at A. Weave the needle through the fabric, making LONG stitches on the top and SHORT stitches on the bottom. Keep stitches even.

---

# Basic Layering Instructions

## Marking Your Quilt:

If you choose to mark your quilt for hand or machine quilting, it is much easier to do so before layering. Press your quilt before you begin. Here are some handy tips regarding marking.

1. A disappearing pen may vanish before you finish.

2. Use a White pencil on dark fabrics.

3. If using a washable Blue pen, remember that pressing may make the pen permanent.

## Pieced Backings:

1. Press the backing fabric before measuring.

2. If possible cut backing fabrics on grain, parallel to the selvage edges.

3. Piece 3 parts rather than 2 whenever possible, sewing 2 side borders to the center. This reduces stress on the pieced seam.

4. The backing and batting should extend at least 2" on each side of the quilt.

## Creating a Quilt Sandwich:

1. Press the backing and top to remove all wrinkles.

2. Lay the backing wrong side up on the table.

3. Position the batting over the backing and smooth out all wrinkles.

4. Center the quilt top over the batting leaving a 2" border all around.

5. Pin the layers together with 2" safety pins positioned a handwidth apart. A grapefruit spoon makes inserting the pins easier. Leaving the pins open in the container speeds up the basting on the next quilt.

# Applique Instructions

## Basic Turned Edge:

1. Trace pattern onto template plastic.

2. Cut out the shape leaving a scant ¼" fabric border all around and clip the curves.

3. Place the template plastic on the wrong side of the fabric. Spray edges with starch.

4. Press the ⅛" border over the edge of the template plastic with the tip of a hot iron. Press firmly.

5. Remove the template, maintaining the folded edge on the back of the fabric.

6. Position the shape on the quilt and Blindstitch in place.

## Basic Needle Turn:

1. Cut out the shape leaving a ¼" fabric border all around.

2. Baste the shapes to the quilt, keeping the basting stitches away from the edge of the fabric.

3. Begin with all areas that are under other layers and work to the topmost layer.

4. For an area no more than 2" ahead of where you are working, trim to ⅛" and clip the curves.

5. Using the needle, roll the edge under and sew tiny Blindstitches to secure.

## Using Fusible Web for Iron-on Applique:

1. Trace the pattern onto *Steam a Seam 2* fusible web.

2. Press the patterns onto the wrong side of the fabric.

3. Cut out patterns exactly on the drawn line.

4. Score the web paper with a pin, then remove the paper.

5. Position the fabric, fusible side down, on the quilt. Press with a hot iron following the fusible web manufacturer's instructions.

6. Stitch around the edge by hand.

Optional: Stabilize the wrong side of the fabric with your favorite stabilizer.

Use a size 80 machine embroidery needle. Fill the bobbin with lightweight basting thread and thread the machine with a machine embroidery thread that complements the color being appliqued.

Set your machine for a Zigzag stitch and adjust the thread tension if needed. Use a scrap to experiment with different stitch widths and lengths until you find the one you like best.

Sew slowly.

# Basic Quilting Instructions

**Hand Quilting:**

Many quilters enjoy the serenity of hand quilting. Because the quilt is handled a great deal, it is important to securely baste the sandwich together. Place the quilt in a hoop and don't forget to hide your knots.

**Machine Quilting:**

All the quilts in this book were machine quilted. Some were quilted on a large, free-arm quilting machine and others were quilted on a sewing machine. If you have never machine quilted before, practice on some scraps first.

**Straight Line Machine Quilting Tips:**

1. Pin baste the layers securely.

2. Set up your sewing machine with a size 80 quilting needle and a walking foot.

3. Experimenting with the decorative stitches on your machine adds interest to your quilt. You do not have to quilt the entire piece with the same stitch. Variety is the spice of life, so have fun trying out stitches you have never used before as well as your favorite stand-bys.

**Free Motion Machine Quilting Tips:**

1. Pin baste the layers securely.

2. Set up your sewing machine with a spring needle, a quilting foot, and lower the feed dogs.

# Basic Mitered Binding Instructions

**A Perfect Finish:**

The binding endures the most stress on a quilt and is usually the first thing to wear out. For this reason, we recommend using a double fold binding.

1. Trim the backing and batting even with the quilt edge.

2. If possible cut strips on the crosswise grain because a little bias in the binding is a Good thing. This is the only place in the quilt where bias is helpful, for it allows the binding to give as it is turned to the back and sewn in place.

3. Strips are usually cut 2½" wide, but check the instructions for your project before cutting.

4. Sew strips end to end to make a long strip sufficient to go all around the quilt plus 4"- 6".

5. With wrong sides together, fold the strip in half lengthwise. Press.

6. Stretch out your hand and place your little finger at the corner of the quilt top. Place the binding where your thumb touches the edge of the quilt. Aligning the edge of the quilt with the raw edges of the binding, pin the binding in place along the first side.

7. Leaving a 2" tail for later use, begin sewing the binding to the quilt with a ¼" seam.

**For Mitered Corners:**

1. Stop ¼" from the first corner. Leave the needle in the quilt and turn it 90°. Hit the reverse button on your machine and back off the quilt leaving the threads connected.

2. Fold the binding perpendicular to the side you sewed, making a 45° angle. Carefully maintaining the first fold, bring the binding back along the edge to be sewn.

3. Carefully align the edges of the binding with the quilt edge and sew as you did the first side. Repeat this process until you reach the tail left at the beginning. Fold the tail out of the way and sew until you are ¼" from the beginning stitches.

4. Remove the quilt from the machine. Fold the quilt out of the way and match the binding tails together. Carefully sew the binding tails with a ¼" seam. You can do this by hand if you prefer.

**Finishing the Binding:**

5. Trim the seam to reduce bulk.

6. Finish stitching the binding to the quilt across the join you just sewed.

7. Turn the binding to the back of the quilt. To reduce bulk at the corners, fold the miter in the opposite direction from which it was folded on the front.

8. Hand-sew a Blind stitch on the back of the quilt to secure the binding in place.

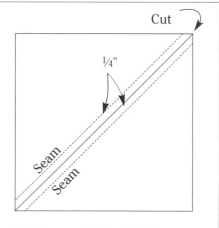

**Half-Square Triangle Diagram**
1. Place 2 squares right sides together.
2. Draw a diagonal line from corner to corner.
3. Stitch ¼" on each side of the line.
4. Cut squares apart on the diagonal line.
5. Open the 2 new squares with 2 colors.
6. Press. Trim off dog-ears.
7. Trim to size.

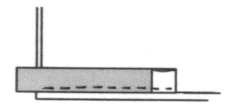

Align the raw edge of the binding with the raw edge of the quilt top. Start about 8" from the corner and go along the first side with a ¼" seam.

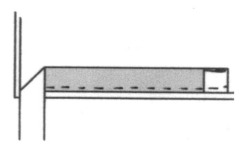

Stop ¼" from the edge. Then stitch a slant to the corner (through both layers of binding)... lift up, then down, as you line up the edge. Fold the binding back.

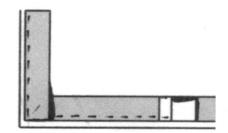

Align the raw edge again. Continue stitching the next side with a ¼" seam as you sew the binding in place.

# Cranberry Wishes Checkerboard Squares

PHOTO ON PAGES 48 - 49

SIZE: 73" x 88"

YARDAGE:
We used a *Moda* "Cranberry Wishes" by Kansas Troubles Quilters
'Jelly Roll' collection of 2½" fabric strips
- we purchased 2 'Jelly Rolls'

| | | |
|---|---|---|
| 1⅛ yards Black | OR | 16 strips |
| 1⅝ yards Light Tan | OR | 22 strips |
| ⅝ yard Cranberry Red | OR | 8 strips |
| ⅝ yard Dark Tan | OR | 8 strips |
| ⅞ yard Dark Olive Green | OR | 12 strips |

| | |
|---|---|
| Border #3 | Purchase ½ yard Black |
| Border #4 & Binding | Purchase 2⅙ yards Cranberry Red print |
| Backing | Purchase 5 yards |
| Batting | Purchase 81" x 96" |

Sewing machine, needle, thread

TIP: You may need to sew smaller strips end to end to enable you to
cut a longer piece. This adds to the charm of the scrappy look.

## CHECKERBOARD CENTERS:
You will need 6 strips each of Dark Tan and Red.
Sew strips together side by side (Red, Dark Tan, Red and Dark Tan)
    to make a strip 8½" x 42". Make 3.
Cut each strip into 2½" x 8½" units (48 total).
Arrange the pieces following the Checkerboard diagram.
    Position columns 1 and 3 with Dark Tan at the top.
    Position columns 2 and 4 with Red at the top.
Sew 4 columns together side by side for each block. Press.
Make 12.

## BORDERS ON CHECKERBOARD BLOCKS:
NOTE: There are 2 borders around EACH Block
    #A Border is the Border for Checkerboard
    #B Border is the Border with Points.

### #A BORDER - for Checkerboard:
**Black**

| Quantity | size | position |
|---|---|---|
| 48 | 2½" x 8½" | Strips for #A Border |

**Dark Tan**

| | | |
|---|---|---|
| 24 | 2½" x 2½" | Corners for #A Border |

**Red**

| | | |
|---|---|---|
| 24 | 2½" x 2½" | Corners for #A Border |

### #B BORDER - with Points:
**Light Tan**

| Quantity | Size | Position |
|---|---|---|
| 48 | 2" x 6½" | Strips for #B Border |
| 48 | 2" x 2" | Corners for #B Border |

NOTE: The Light Tan borders are cut 2".

## BLOCK ASSEMBLY:
### #A BORDER - for Checkerboard:
SIDES:
Sew a Black 2½" x 8½" strip to each side of a checkerboard unit.
    Press.

TOP AND BOTTOM:
Sew a 2½" square to each end of 24 Black 2½" x 8½" strips. Press.
    (12 will have Dark Tan squares and 12 will have Red squares).
    Sew these strips to the top and bottom of each checkerboard unit.
    Press.

Piano Keys
Sew 4 strips
together
side by side.

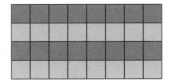

Cut strips into
2½" x 8½" units.

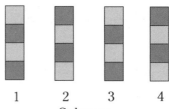

| 1 | 2 | 3 | 4 |
|---|---|---|---|

Columns -
You will need 48 units.

Checkerboard Center.
Finished block - 8½" x 8½"
Make 12.

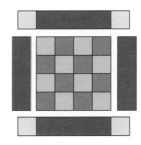

#A Border
Add the side strips.

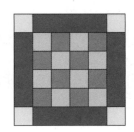

#A Border
Add the top and
bottom strips.
Finished Checkerboard
Block - 12½" x 12½"

Each pair of squares
will makes 2
Half-Square Triangles

**#B BORDER - with Points:**
**HALF-SQUARE TRIANGLES:**
TIP: Refer to Half-Square Triangle instructions on page 24.
You will make 192 Black/Light Tan Half-Square Triangles
    (16 for each of 12 blocks).
You will need 6 strips each of Black and Light Tan.
Place a Black strip and Light Tan strip right sides together,
    align the strips carefully.
With the Light Tan strip on top, cut 96 squares 2½" x 2½".

    Pair up two 2½" x 2½" colors together.
    Draw a line from corner to corner on the diagonal.
    Sew a seam ¼" on each side of the diagonal line.
    Cut apart on the diagonal line to make 2 squares.
    Press.
    Make 192 Half-Square Triangles.
    Center and trim each Half-Square Triangle to 2" x 2".

Sew a corner square
to each end.
Make 24 Strip Units

#B Border
Make 48
Strip Units

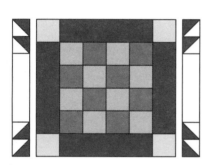

#B Borders
Add the side strip units.

Add the top and bottom
strip units.

**STRIP UNITS:**

Sew 2 Half-Square Triangles on each side of 48 Tan 2" x 6½" strips.
    TIP: Be sure to position the diagonal in the correct direction.
    Press. Make 48.

**SIDE BORDERS:**
NOTE: Seams will only align at the corner squares on this border.
    Sew one strip unit to each side of 12 blocks.
    Press.

**TOP AND BOTTOM BORDERS:**
NOTE: Seams will only align at the corner squares on this border.
    Sew a 2" x 2" Light Tan corner square to each end of 24 Strip Units.
    Sew a Strip Unit to the top and bottom of each block.
    Press.
Each block will measure 15½" x 15½" at this point.

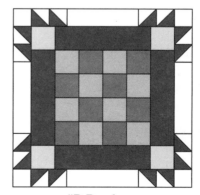

#B Borders
Finished Block - 15½" x 15½"

Row 1

Row 2

Row 3

Row 4

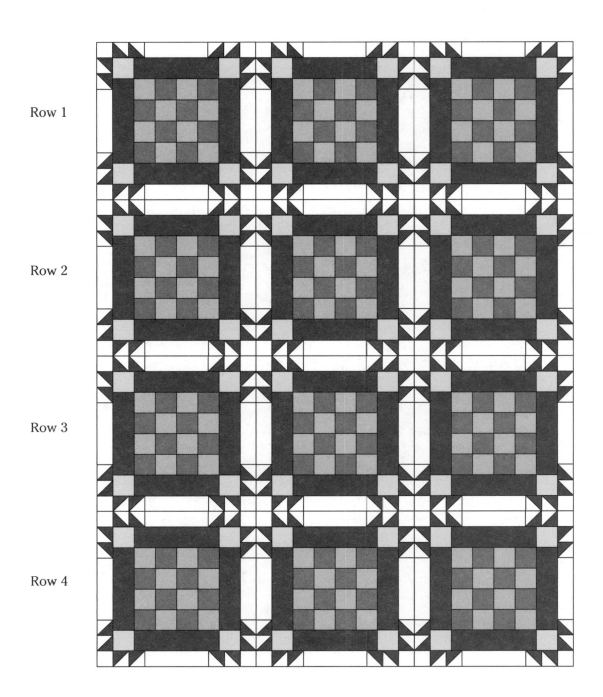

ASSEMBLY:
Arrange all 12 Blocks on a work surface or table.
Refer to diagram for block placement and direction.
Sew blocks together in 4 rows, 3 blocks per row. Press.
Sew rows together. Press.
The quilt will measure 45½" x 60½".

Cranberry Wishes
Quilt Assembly

OUTER BORDERS:

**Light Tan Pieced Scrappy Border #1:**
Sew leftover Light Tan strips together end to end.
  Cut 2 strips 2½" x 60½" for sides.
  Cut 2 strips 2½" x 49½" for top and bottom.
  Sew side borders to the quilt. Press.
  Sew top and bottom borders to the quilt. Press.

**Dark Olive Green Pieced Scrappy Border #2:**
Sew 6 Olive Green strips together end to end.
Sew 6 more Olive Green strips together end to end.
  Sew these 2 long strips together side by side.
Cut 2 strips 4½" x 64½" for sides.
Cut 2 strips 4½" x 57½" for top and bottom.
Sew side borders to the quilt. Press.
Sew top and bottom borders to the quilt. Press.

**Black Border #3:**
Cut 7 strips 2½" x the width of fabric.
  Sew strips together end to end.
Cut 2 strips 2½" x 72½" for sides.
Cut 2 strips 2½" x 61½" for top and bottom.
  Sew side borders to the quilt. Press.
  Sew top and bottom borders to the quilt. Press.

**Border #4:**
TIP: Cut border strips parallel to the fabric selvage to eliminate piecing.
Cut 2 strips 6½" x 76½" for sides.
Cut 2 strips 6½" x 73½" for top and bottom.
  Sew side borders to the quilt. Press.
  Sew top and bottom borders to the quilt. Press.

FINISHING:
**Quilting**:
  See Basic Instructions on pages 24 - 26.
**Binding**:
  Cut strips 2½" wide.
  Sew together end to end to equal 332".
  See Binding Instructions on page 26.

# Peace on Earth Blocks

PHOTO ON PAGES 4 - 5

SIZE: 67" x 82"

YARDAGE:
We used a *Moda* "Peace on Earth" by 3 Sisters
'Jelly Roll' collection of 2½" fabric strips
- we purchased 2 'Jelly Rolls'

| | | |
|---|---|---|
| ¾ yard Cranberry Red | OR | 10 strips |
| 1¼ yards Tan | OR | 17 strips |
| ⅔ yard Light Green | OR | 9 strips |
| ⅝ yard Brown | OR | 8 strips |
| ⅞ yard Blue Gray | OR | 12 strips |

| | |
|---|---|
| Border #3 | Purchase ⅓ yard Brown |
| Border #4 & Binding | Purchase 2 yards Green-Brown print |
| Backing | Purchase 5 yards |
| Batting | Purchase 75" x 90" |

Sewing machine, needle, thread

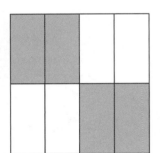

Center Stripes
for Block A

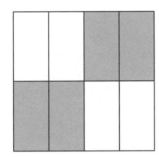

Center Stripes
for Block B

## PREPARATION FOR BLOCKS
### BLOCKS A - B - C - D:
**Center Stripes for Block A and B:**

Make 1 of A and 1 of B.
Cut 2 Blue strips and 2 Tan strips 18" long.
Sew the Blue strips together side by side to make a piece
    4½" x 18".
Repeat for the Tan strips.
Cut each strip into 4½" x 4½" pieces. You need 4, (2 of each) for
    each block.
Arrange the pieces following the Block A & B diagrams.
Sew 2 rows of 2 pieces for each block. Press.
Sew the rows together. Press.

Center
Stripe Unit
for Blocks
C & D

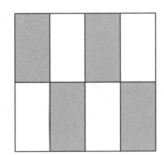

Stripes
for Block C

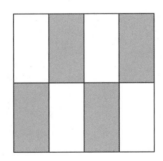

Stripes
for Block D

**Center Stripe Unit for Blocks C & D:**

Make 2 of each block.
Sew a Blue strip and a Tan strip together side by
    side to make a piece 4½" x 36". Make 2.
Cut each strip into 4½" x 4½" pieces. You need 16,
    4 for each block.
Arrange the pieces following the Block C and
    Block D diagrams.
Sew 2 rows of 2 pieces each for each block. Press.
Sew the rows together. Press.

Cut 24 Brown strips 2½" x 8½".
Sew to left and right sides.

Sew a Light Green square to each end
of the remaining 12 Brown strips.
Sew to top and bottom.

**Inner Border for Blocks A, B, C and D:**
Cut 24 Brown strips 2½" x 8½". You will need 4 per block.
Sew a strip to the left and right sides of 6 Center Stripes section. Press.

Cut 24 Light Green squares 2½" x 2½".
Sew a Light Green square to each end of the remaining 12 Brown strips. Press.
Sew a strip to the top and bottom of 6 Center Stripes section. Press.

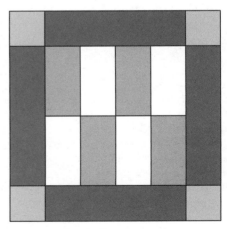

Inner Border
for Blocks A, B, C & D

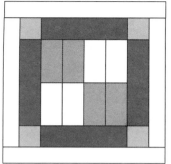

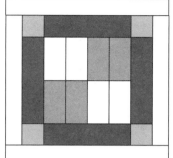

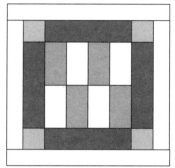

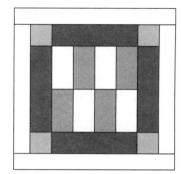

| Block A - Make 1 | Block B - Make 1 | Block C - Make 2 | Block D - Make 2 |
|---|---|---|---|

**Tan Outer Border for
Blocks A, B, C and D:**
Cut 12 Tan strips 2' x 12½" for the sides of each block.
Cut 12 Tan strips 2' x 15½" for the top and bottom of each block.
Sew the side strips to the block. Press.
Sew the top and bottom strips to each block. Press.

Each pair of squares
will makes 2
Half-Square Triangles

BLOCKS E - F - G:

**Half-Square Triangles:**
TIP: Refer to Half-Square Triangle instructions on page 24.
You will make 112 Red/Tan half-square triangles.

For each color, sew 4 strips end to end to make 140".
Trim the excess and set aside for use in another block.

Place the Red strip and Tan strip right sides together, aligning carefully.
Cut 56 squares 2½" x 2½".

    Pair up two 2½" x 2½" colors together.
    Draw a line from corner to corner on the diagonal.
    Sew a seam ¼" on each side of the diagonal line.
    Cut apart on the diagonal line to make 2 squares. Press.
    Make 112 Half-Square Triangles.
    Center and trim each Half-Square Triangle to 2" x 2".

Set aside the following Half-Square Triangles for these blocks:
    64 for 2 of Block E
    16 for 2 of Block F
    32 for 2 of Block G

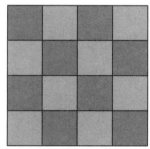

**Checkerboard Block Centers:**
Make 6.
Sew 3 Blue strips end to end. Cut 2 pieces 60" long.
Sew 3 Brown strips end to end. Cut 2 pieces 60" long.
Sew Blue - Brown - Blue - Brown strips side by side to make a piece 8½" x 60".
Cut each strip into 2½" x 8½" pieces. You need 24, 4 for each block.
Arrange the pieces following the Checkerboard diagram.
Sew the rows together. Press.

Checkerboard Center
for Blocks E, F, & G

**Inner Border for Checkerboard Blocks:**
Cut 24 Red strips 2½" x 8½". You will need 4 per block.
Sew a strip to each side of the checkerboard section. Press.
Cut 24 Light Green squares 2½" x 2½".
Sew a Light Green square to each end of the 12 Red strips.
    Press.
Sew a strip to the top and bottom of the checkerboard
    section. Press.

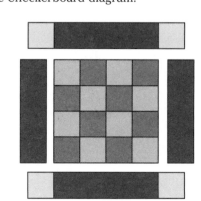

Inner Border
for Blocks E, F & G

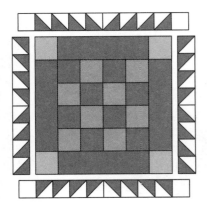

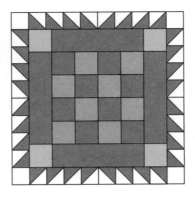

Block E - Make 2

## PREPARATION FOR BLOCKS

**Border for Block E:**
You'll need 64 half-square triangles.
Cut 8 Tan squares 2" x 2" for the corners.
Following Block 1 Diagram, position 8 half-square triangles
    for each side, noting the direction of the diagonal.
**Sides:**
Sew 8 half-square triangles together to make strips 12½"
    long. Press. Make 4.
Sew the sides to the block. Press.
**Top and Bottom:**
Sew 8 half-square triangles into a 12½" strip. Press. Make 4.
    Sew a Tan square to each end. Press.
    Sew the top and bottom borders to the block. Press.
Make 2 of Block E.

**Border for Block F:**
You'll need 16 half-square triangles.
Cut 8 Red rectangles 2 x 5½" for the sides.
Cut 8 Tan rectangles 2" x 2½" for the sides.
Cut 8 Tan rectangles 2" x 4" for the top and bottom.
**For each Border Section:**
    Noting the direction of the diagonal, sew a half-square
    triangle to each end of Red 5½" strips. Press. Make 8.
**Sides:**
Sew a 2" x 2½" Tan piece to each end of 4 border sections.
    Press.
    Sew the sides to the block. Press.
**Top and Bottom:**
Sew a Tan 2" x 4" to each end of the border section. Press.
    Sew the borders to the block. Press.
Make 2 of Block F.

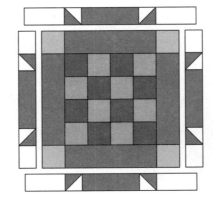

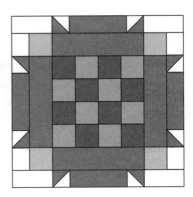

Block F - Make 2

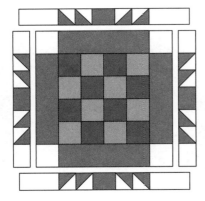

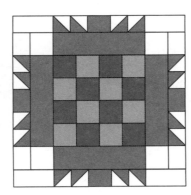

Block G - Make 2

**Border for Block G:**
You'll need 16 half-square triangles.
Cut 8 Red rectangles 2 x 2½" for the sides.
Cut 8 Tan rectangles 2" x 2½" for the sides.
Cut 8 Tan rectangles 2" x 4" for the top and bottom.
**For each Border Section:**
    Sew 2 half-square triangles to each end of Red 2½"
    strips, noting diagonal direction. Press. Make 8.
**Sides:**
    Sew a 2" x 2½" Tan piece to each end of 4 border
    sections. Press.
    Sew the sides to the block. Press.
**Top and Bottom:**
    Sew a Tan 2" x 4" to each end of 4 border sections.
    Press.
    Sew the borders to the block. Press.
Make 2 of block G.

Each block will measure 15½" x 15½" at this point.

## ASSEMBLY:
    Arrange all Blocks on a work surface or table.
    Refer to diagram for block placement and direction.
        Row 1: Block E, Block A, Block F
        Row 2: Block C, Block G, Block D
        Row 3: Block F, Block B upside down, Block E
        Row 4: Block D, Block G, Block C
    Sew blocks together in 4 rows, 3 blocks per row. Press.
    Sew rows together. Press.

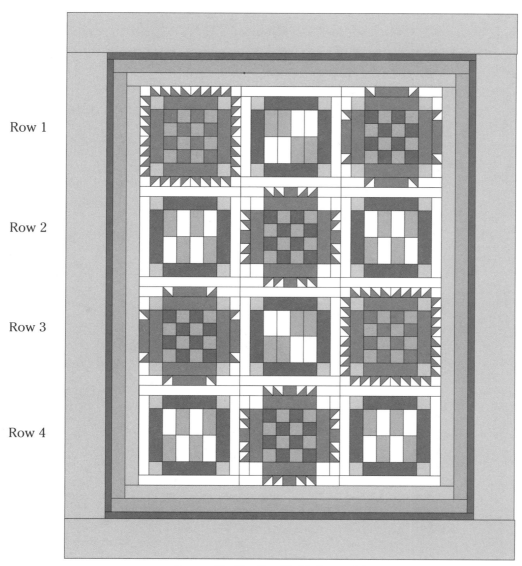

Peace On Earth - Quilt Assembly

**BORDERS:**

**Green Pieced Border #1:**
Sew leftover Green strips together end to end.
>Cut 2 strips 2½" x 60½" for sides.
>Cut 2 strips 2½" x 49½" for top and bottom.
>Sew side borders to the quilt. Press.
>Sew top and bottom borders to the quilt. Press.

**Blue Pieced Border #2:**
Sew leftover Blue strips together end to end.
>Cut 2 strips 2½" x 64½" for sides.
>Cut 2 strips 2½" x 53½" for top and bottom.
>Sew side borders to the quilt. Press.
>Sew top and bottom borders to the quilt. Press.

**Border #3:**
Cut 6 strips 1½" by the width of fabric .
Sew strips together end to end.
>Cut 2 strips 1½" x 68½" for sides.
>Cut 2 strips 1½" x 55½" for top and bottom.
>Sew side borders to the quilt. Press.
>Sew bottom borders to the quilt. Press.

**Border #4:**
TIP: Cut the strips parallel to the selvage to eliminate piecing on the long borders.
>Cut 2 strips 6½" x 70½" for sides.
>Cut 2 strips 6½" x 67½" for top and bottom.
>Sew side borders to the quilt. Press.
>Sew top and bottom borders to the quilt. Press.

FINISHING:
**Quilting**:
>See Basic Instructions on pages 24 - 26.
**Binding**:
>Cut strips 2½" wide.
>Sew together end to end to equal 308".
>See Binding Instructions on page 26.

# Fresh Squeezed Tulips

PHOTO ON PAGES 46 - 47

SIZE: 62" x 70"

YARDAGE:

We used a *Moda* "Fresh Squeezed" by Sandy Gervais
'Jelly Roll' collection of 2½" fabric strips
- we purchased 1 'Jelly Roll'

| | | |
|---|---|---|
| ⅙ yard Turquoise | OR | 3 strips |
| ⅝ yard Red | OR | 5 strips |
| ½ yard Orange | OR | 6 strips |
| ½ yard Green | OR | 7 strips |
| ⅔ yard Yellow | OR | 8 strips |
| ¾ yard Cream | OR | 10 strips |

| | |
|---|---|
| Border #1 | Purchase ½ yard Lime Green |
| Border #2 & Binding | Purchase 2 yards Yellow print |
| Backing | Purchase 4 yards |
| Batting | Purchase 70" x 78" |

Sewing machine, needle, thread

TIP: I used only 1 strip of each color (plaid, stripe or print) to create the patterns in the flowers. The flowers also look great with all prints in a color.

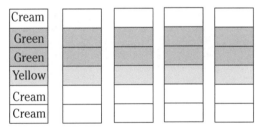

Cut strip sections 4½" x 12½"

LEAF SECTIONS:

Cut the following strips 36" long:
 6 Cream
 4 Green
 2 Light Yellow

Sew the following strips together to make a piece 12½" x 36":
 1 Cream - 2 Green - 1 Light Yellow - 2 Cream

Repeat for the remaining strips.

From these pieces cut 16 strip sections 4½" x 12½".

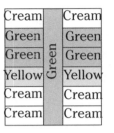

| Stem and Leaf | Stem and Leaf |
|---|---|
| for flowers A, C, F, & H | for flowers B, D, E, & G |

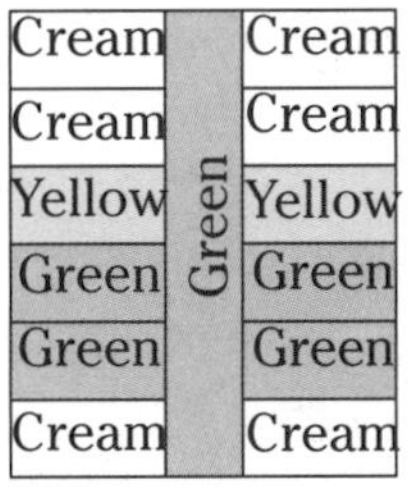

STEM and LEAF BLOCKS:

NOTE:

The sections for flowers A, C, F, and H have strip sections with 1 Cream strip at the top.

The sections for flowers B, D, E and G turn the strip sections upside down so there are 2 Cream strips at the top.

Cut 8 Green stems 2½" x 12½".

Sew 4 blocks with a set of strip sections on each side of the stem (aligning 1 Cream strip at the top). Press. Label these block A, C, F, and H.

Sew 4 blocks with a set of strip sections on each side of the stem (aligning 2 Cream strips at the top). Press. Label these block B, D, E, and G.

CUTTING CHART:

TIP: All strips are 2½" wide by the indicated measurement. Label the pieces as you cut.

TIP: You may need to sew smaller strips end to end to enable you to cut a longer piece. This adds to the charm of the scrappy look.

**Cream**

| Quantity | Length | |
|---|---|---|
| 8 | 10½" | Top of each flower block |
| 8 | 4½" | Center top of each flower |
| 32 | 2½" | Outer bottom corners and center top of each flower |

**Orange**

| | | |
|---|---|---|
| 6 | 26½" | Vertical sashing |
| 4 | 10½" | Horizontal sashing |

**Red**

| | | |
|---|---|---|
| 12 | 10½" | 4 each for flowers A, D & F |
| 3 | 8½" | 1 each for flowers A, D & F (centers) |

**Turquoise**

| | | |
|---|---|---|
| 4 | 10½" | 2 each for flowers B & H |
| 4 | 6½" | 2 each for flowers B & H |
| 2 | 4½" | 1 each for flowers B & H |
| 6 | 4½" | 3 each for flowers B & H (centers) |

**Yellow**

| | | |
|---|---|---|
| 8 | 10½" | 4 each for flowers C & E |
| 2 | 8½" | 1 each for flowers C & E (centers) |
| 4 | 10½" | 4 for flower G |
| 1 | 8½" | 1 for flower G |

**Green**

| | | |
|---|---|---|
| 3 | 2½" | Cornerstones |

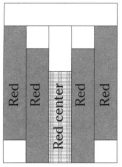

Flowers A, D & F
Make 3

## FLOWER SECTIONS:
### Flowers A, D, and F - RED:
Sew a Cream 2½" square to one end of each 10½" Red strip. Press.
Sew a Cream 4½" strip to the 8½" Red (center) strip. Press.
Arrange the pieces following the diagram and sew the 5 strips together side by side.
  Press.
Sew a 10½" Cream strip to the top of the block. Press.
  Make 3.

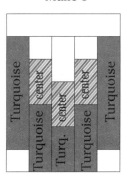

Flowers B & H
Make 2

### Flowers B and H - TURQUOISE:
**Side Columns 1 & 5:** Sew a Cream 2½" square to one end of each 10½" Turquoise strip (side). Press.
**Mid Columns 2 & 4:** Sew a 6½" Turquoise - 4½" Turquoise (center) - 2½" Cream square. Press.
**Center Column 3:** Sew a 4½" Turquoise - 4½" Turquoise (center) Stripe - 4½" Cream strip. Press.
Sew columns 1-2-3-4-5 together side by side. Press.
Sew a 10½" Cream strip to the top of the block. Press.
  Make 2.

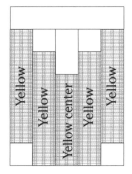

Flower C, E & G
Make 3

### Flower C, E & G - YELLOW:
Sew a Cream 2½" square to one end of each 10½" Yellow strip. Press.
Sew a Cream 4½" strip to each 8½" Yellow strip. Press.
Arrange the pieces following the diagram and sew the 5 strips together. Press.
Sew a 10½" Cream strip to the top of the block. Press.
  Make 3.

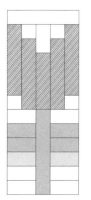

1 Cream strip at the
top of Leaf Block

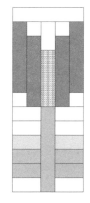

2 Cream strips at the
top of Leaf Block

## ASSEMBLE THE FLOWER BLOCKS:
Sew a Flower to each Stem and Leaf Block.
Sew flowers A, C, F, and H to blocks with
  1 Cream strip at the top.
Sew flowers B, D, E and G to blocks with
  2 Cream strips at the top.
Each block will measure 10½" x 26½" at this point.

## SASHING:
### Horizontal Sashing or the Center Row:
Sew sashing row together using strips and cornerstones:
  Orange strip - Green square - Orange strip - Green square - Orange strip - Green square - Orange strip

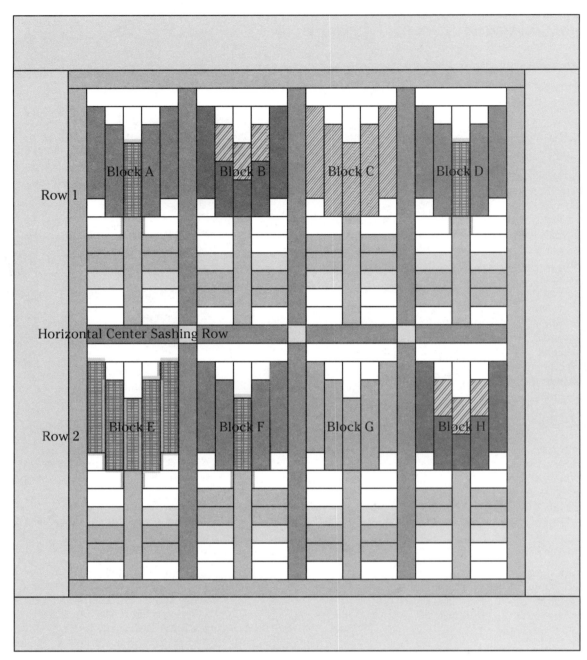

Fresh Squeezed Tulips - Quilt Assembly

ASSEMBLY:
Arrange all Blocks on a work surface or table.
Refer to diagram for block placement.
Sew blocks together in 2 rows, 4 blocks per row with an Orange vertical sashing strip between each block. Press.
Sew the horizontal center sashing strip to the bottom of row 1. Press.
Sew rows together. Press.

BORDERS:
**Border #1:**
Cut 6 strips 2½" x 42" by the width of fabric.
Sew strips together end to end.
Cut 2 strips 2½" x 54½" for sides.
Cut 2 strips 2½" x 50½" for top and bottom.
Sew side borders to the quilt. Press.
Sew top and bottom borders to the quilt. Press.

**Border #2:**
Cut the strips parallel to the selvage to eliminate piecing on the long borders.
Cut 2 strips 6½" x 58½" for sides.
Cut 2 strips 6½" x 62½" for top and bottom.
Sew side borders to the quilt. Press.
Sew top and bottom borders to the quilt. Press.

FINISHING:
**Quilting:**
See Basic Instructions on pages 24 - 26.
**Binding:**
Cut strips 2½" wide.
Sew together end to end to equal 274".
See Binding Instructions on page 26.

# Birchwood Lane House

SIZE:    80" x 86" with the Log Cabin border
        44" x 50" without the Log Cabin border

YARDAGE:

We used a *Moda* "Birchwood Lane" by Holly Taylor
'Jelly Roll' collection of 2½" fabric strips

SMALL LAP QUILT without a Log Cabin border:
    You need to purchase 1 Jelly Roll for the quilt
Strips Needed for the small quilt:

| | | |
|---|---|---|
| ⅓ yard Light Brown | OR | 4 strips |
| ⅓ yard Dark Brown | OR | 4 strips |
| ½ yard Light Green | OR | 6 strips |
| ½ yard Dark Green | OR | 6 strips |
| ⅝ yard Red | OR | 8 strips |
| ½ yard Tan | OR | 7 strips |
| ⅙ yard Cream | OR | 2 strips |

Binding for Small        Purchase ⅜ yard Red
Backing for Small        Purchase 3 yards
Batting for Small        Purchase 52" x 58"
Sewing machine, needle, thread
*DMC* Dark Green pearl cotton or embroidery floss
#22 or #24 Chenille needle

LARGE BED QUILT with a Log Cabin border:
    You need to purchase 2 Jelly Rolls for the quilt and Log
    Cabin border.
Additional Strips Needed for the Log Cabin border:

| | | |
|---|---|---|
| ¼ yard Light Brown | OR | 3 strips |
| ⅓ yard Dark Brown | OR | 4 strips |
| ½ yard Light Green | OR | 7 strips |
| ½ yard Dark Green | OR | 6 strips |
| ⅝ yard Red | OR | 8 strips |
| ⅜ yard Tan | OR | 5 strips |

Border #1 for Large      Purchase ½ yard Dark Brown
Border #2 & Binding      Purchase 2½ yards Red
Backing for Large        Purchase 4 yards
Batting for large        Purchase 88" x 94"

## PREPARATION FOR BLOCKS:

Chimney

**Roof and Chimney Section:**
    Cut 1 Cream strip 2½" x 16½".
    Cut 2 Tan strips 2½" x 16½".
    Cut 2 Dark Brown strips 2½" x 16½" (roof).
    Cut 1 Dark Brown strip 2½" x 12½" (roof).
    Cut 3 Tan strips 2½" x 4½".
    Cut 2 Dark Brown squares 2½" x 2½".
    Cut 2 Tan squares 2½" x 2½" (roof).

**Chimney:**
    Sew the following strips end to end:
        4½" Tan - 2½" Brown - 4½" Tan - 2½" Brown - 4½" Tan.
        Press.
    Sew 2 Tan and 1 Cream strip to the top of the section.
        Press.

Roof
Section

**Roof:**
    Sew a Tan square to each end of the 12½" Dark
        Brown strip. Press.
    Sew 2 Dark Brown 16½" strips to the bottom of the
        section. Press.

**Roof Assembly:**
    Sew the Chimney section to the Roof section. Press.

Window Section        Door        Window Section

**House Window Sections:**
    Cut 4 Red strips 2½" x 14½".
    Cut 4 Red strips 2½" x 4½".
    Cut 2 Red squares 2½" x 2½".
    Cut 4 Dark Brown squares 2½" x 2½".
    Sew a Dark Brown square to each end of 1 Red square.
        Press.
        Make 2.
    Sew a Red 2½" x 4½" to each end of the 2 pieces. Press.
    Sew a Red 14½" strip to each side of the 2 pieces. Press.

**House Door Section:**
    Cut 2 Dark Brown strips 2½" x 6½" for the door.
    Cut 1 Dark Brown and 3 Red strips 2½" x 4½".
    Sew the 4½" strips together side by side Red-Red-Brown-
        Red to make a piece 4½" x 8½". Press.
    Sew the 6½" Brown strips together side by side
        to make a door 4½" x 6½". Press.
    Sew the door to the Red-Red-Brown-Red section.
        Press.

**House Assembly:**
**Assemble the House:**
    Sew a Window section-
        Door section-Window
        section.
        Press.

**Center Assembly:**
    Sew the Chimney and the
        Roof sections to the
        House section.
        Press.

**Top and Bottom Borders:**
Cut 2 Cream strips 2½" x 16½".
    Sew 1 to the top and 1 to the
        bottom of the House
        Section.
    Press.

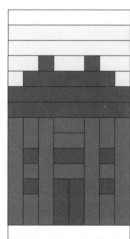

House Assembly

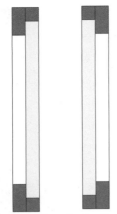

Left Side Border · Right Side Border

## Quilt Center:
### House Side borders:
Cut 4 Red strips 2½" x 4½".
Cut 4 Red squares 2½" x 2½".
Cut 2 Cream strips 2½" x 22½".
Cut 2 Tan strips 2½" x 26½".
Sew a Red 2½" x 4½" to each end of the 2 Cream strips.
Sew a Red square to each end of the 2 Tan strips. Press.
Sew each Cream strip to a Tan strip to make a left and right border. Press.

### House Side Borders:
Sew the left and right borders to the house. Press.

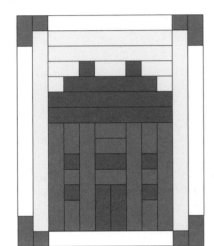

Borders Assembly

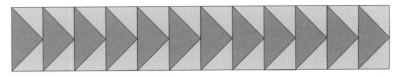

(6) Flying Geese Border Diagram - Make 2

(6) Refer to the Flying Geese Border diagram.
Sew 12 Geese units together with the triangles pointing to the right to make a piece 4½" x 24½". Press. Make 2.

### Sew Borders:
Sew a strip with the Geese pointing to the right to the top of the quilt center. Press.
Sew a strip with the Geese point to the left to the bottom of the quilt center. Press.

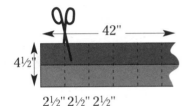

42"

4½"

2½" 2½" 2½"

Checkerboard Sections - Make 16

## Make the Checkerboard:
You need 2 Dark Brown and 2 Light Brown strips, each 2½" x 42".
Sew 1 Dark Brown to 1 Light Brown strip together side by side to make 4½" x 42".
Repeat with the other 2 strips.

### Cut into Sections:
Cut strips into 16 sections 2½" x 4½".
Cut 1 Light Brown square 2½" x 2½"
Cut 1 Dark Brown square 2½" x 2½".

### Left Border:
Sew 9 checkerboard 2-color sections end to end, Dark Brown-Light Brown. Press.
Sew a Dark Brown square to one end. Press.
Sew border to the left side of the quilt center. Press.

### Right Border:
Sew 9 checkerboard 2-color sections end to end, Light Brown-Dark Brown. Press.
Sew a Light Brown square to one end. Press.
Sew border to the right side of the quilt center. Press.

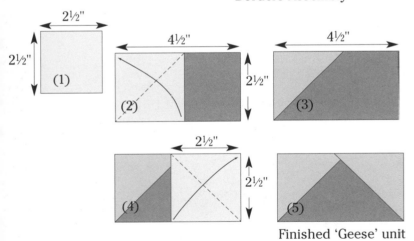

(1) 2½" x 2½"

(2) 4½" x 2½"

(3) 4½"

(4) 2½"

(5) 2½"

Finished 'Geese' unit

## Flying Geese:
Make 24.
Cut 24 Dark Green rectangles 2½" x 4½".
(1) Cut 48 Light Green squares 2½" x 2½".
Refer to the Flying Geese Construction diagrams.
(2) Place a Dark Green rectangle with right side up. With right sides together, position a Light Green square on top, (on the left) aligning the edges.
(3) Draw a diagonal line as shown. Sew on the line. Fold back the triangle. Press.
Trim away excess fabric underneath to decrease the bulk in the quilt top.
(4) Position the second Light Green square (on the right). Draw a diagonal, noting the direction of the diagonal.
(5) Sew on the diagonal, fold back. Press and trim as before.

Make 2

## Top and Bottom Borders:
Sew 7 checkerboard 2-color sections end to end, Light Brown-Dark Brown. Press. Make 2.
Sew a border to the top and a border to the bottom of the quilt center. Press.

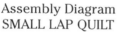 *Birchwood House* continued

Assembly Diagram
SMALL LAP QUILT

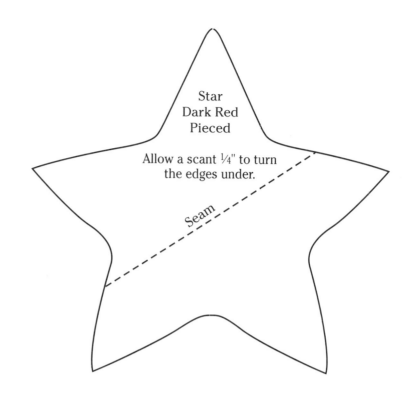

Star
Dark Red
Pieced

Allow a scant ¼" to turn
the edges under.

Seam

## Border #1 - Green, Light Green & Red:

### Side Borders:
Cut 2 Light Green strips 42½" long.
Cut 2 Dark Green strips 42½" long.
Cut 2 Red side strips 42½" long.
Sew strips together side by side to make a
 piece 6½" x 42½" for the sides.
 Red-Dark Green-Light Green
 Press. Make 2.
Sew side borders to the quilt.
 Press.

### Top and Bottom Borders:
Cut 2 Red strips 2½" x 40½".
Sew top and bottom borders to the quilt.
 Press.

## Border #2 - Tan & Light Brown:
Cut 2 Tan side strips 30½" long.
 Label these strips "side borders".
Cut 2 Tan top and bottom strips 28½" long.
 Label these strips "top and bottom".
Cut 8 Light Brown strips 8½" long.

### Sew Borders:
Sew a Light Brown strip to each end
 of all 4 Tan strips. Press.
Sew side borders to the quilt.
 Press.
Sew top and bottom borders to the quilt.
 Press.

**Bird Beak**

Cut a Cream 1½" square. Fold
it three times to form a beak
shape. Press each fold. Tuck the
raw edge under the bird body.

Wing
Dark Green
Make 1

**Turned Edge
Applique:**

Allow a scant
¼" to turn the
edges under
(on all pieces).

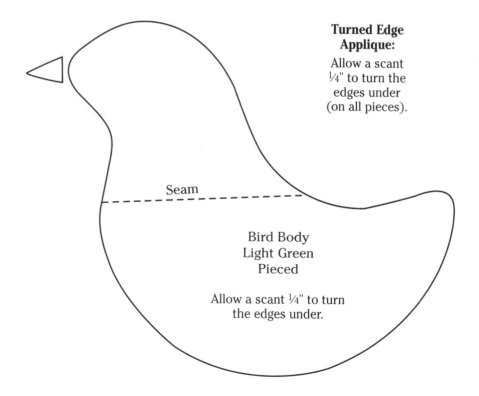

Seam

Bird Body
Light Green
Pieced

Allow a scant ¼" to turn
the edges under.

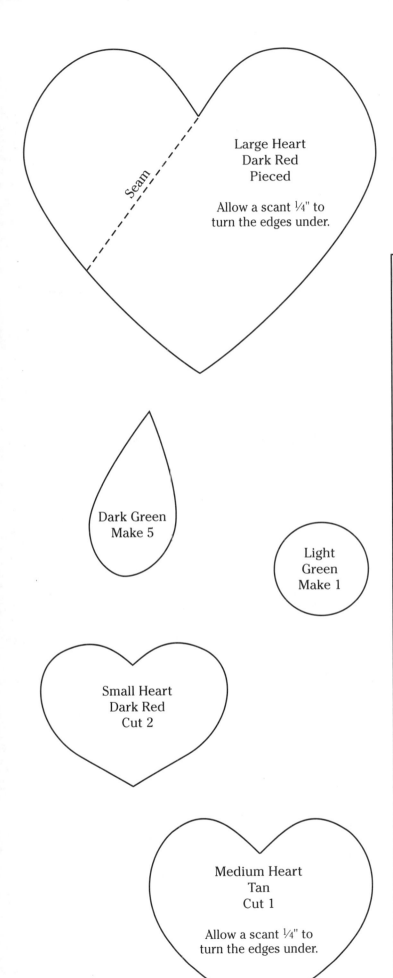

**Large Heart**
**Dark Red**
**Pieced**

*Seam*

Allow a scant ¼" to
turn the edges under.

**Dark Green**
**Make 5**

**Light**
**Green**
**Make 1**

**Small Heart**
**Dark Red**
**Cut 2**

**Medium Heart**
**Tan**
**Cut 1**

Allow a scant ¼" to
turn the edges under.

**APPLIQUES (optional):**
Refer to diagram for placement and embroidered vines.
Cut 2 Red strips 2½" x 8½" long. Sew them together
side by side to make a piece 4½" x 8½". Press.
Cut out Star and Large Heart, note placement of seam.
Cut out remaining designs.
Follow the Applique Instructions on page 23.
**Bird Beak:** Cut a Cream 1" square. Fold it twice to
shape like a beak and tuck it under the bird.

Applique all pieces in place.

**SMALL LAP QUILT:**
You can stop here and bind the edge for a beautiful
44" x 50" lap quilt.

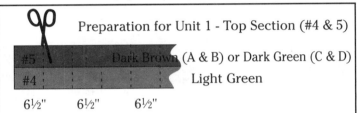

Preparation for Unit 1 - Top Section (#4 & 5)

#5    Dark Brown (A & B) or Dark Green (C & D)
#4    Light Green

6½"       6½"       6½"

**LARGE BED QUILT:**
Add a Log Cabin border to make a larger quilt.
**Modified Log Cabin Border:**
**Preparation for Unit 1 - Top Section:**
Light Green - You need 2 strips 2½" x 42" for #4.
Light Green - You need 2 strips 2½" x 26" for #4.
Dark Green - You need 2 strips 2½" x 42" for #5.
Dark Green - You need 1 strip 2½" x 26" for #5.
Light Brown - You need 1 strip 2½" x 26" for #5.
Sew strips together side by side to make pieces 4½" wide:
Sew 2 Lt Green/Dk Green pieces 2½" x 42".
Sew 1 Lt Green/Dk Green piece 2½" x 26"
Sew 1 Lt Green/Lt Brown piece 2½" x 26"
Cut into 20 units 4½" x 6½":
(16 Lt Green/Dk Green and 4 Lt Green/Lt Brown).

**CUTTING FOR MODIFIED LOG CABIN BORDER:**

Tip: All strips are 2½" wide by the indicated length.

Tip: Cut the longest strips first.
Label the pieces as you cut and group by Block.

Tip: When needed sew smaller strips end to end to enable you to
cut a longer piece. This adds to the charm of the scrappy look.

**Light Brown**

| Quantity | Length | Position |
|---|---|---|
| 8 | 8½" | 2 for A-#6 and 2 for B-#6 |
| | | 2 for E-#6 and 2 for E-#7 |
| 2 | 6½" | 2 for E-#5 |

**Dark Brown**

| | | |
|---|---|---|
| 10 | 10½" | 2 for A-#8 and 2 for B-#8 |
| | | 2 for E-#8 |
| | | 4 for top and bottom borders |
| 4 | 6½" | 2 for A-#7 and 2 for B-#7 |

**Dark Green**

| | | |
|---|---|---|
| 16 | 8½" | 8 for C-#6 and 8 for D-#6 |

**Red**

| | | |
|---|---|---|
| 16 | 10½" | 8 for C-#8 and 8 for D-#8 |
| 16 | 8½" | 8 for C-#7 and 8 for D-#7 |

**Light Green**

| | | |
|---|---|---|
| 8 | 6½" | 4 for E-#3 and 4 for E-#4 |
| 2 | 2½" | 2 for E-#1 |

**Tan**

| | | |
|---|---|---|
| 2 | 4½" | 2 for E-#2 |

*Birchwood House* continued

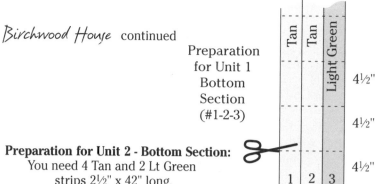

Preparation
for Unit 1
Bottom
Section
(#1-2-3)

Tan | Tan | Light Green

4½"

4½"

4½"

1 | 2 | 3

**Preparation for Unit 2 - Bottom Section:**
You need 4 Tan and 2 Lt Green
strips 2½" x 42" long.
You need 2 Tan and 1 Lt Green
strips 2½" x 9" long.

Sew 2 Tan and 1 Lt Green 2½" x 42" strips together side by
side: Tan-Tan-Lt Green to make 6½" x 42½".
Repeat for the remaining strips.
Cut into sections 4½" x 6½". You need 20 pieces.

Sew 2 Tan and 1 Lt Green 2½" x 9' strips together side by
side: Tan-Tan-Lt Green to make 6½" x 9". Press.
Cut into 2 sections 4½" x 6½". You will have 2 pieces.

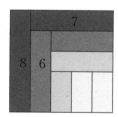

Unit 1 for A & C
Make 2 of A (Lt Brown/Lt Green)
Make 8 of C (Dk Green/Lt Green)

Top
Section

Bottom
Section

Unit 1 for B & D
Make 2 of B (Lt Brown/Lt Green)
Make 8 of D (Dk Green/Lt Green)

**Unit 1 - Bottom Section:**
**Unit 1 for Blocks A & C:** Make 10.
Unit 1-A & 1-C, see position of colors: Light Green-Tan-Tan.
Sew a Top #4-5 strip to the top of Bottom #1-2-3. Press.
Label 2 pieces A and 8 pieces C.

**Unit 1 for Blocks B & D:** Make 10.
Unit 1-B & 1-D, see position of colors: Tan-Tan-Light Green.
Sew a Top #4-5 strip to the top of Bottom #1-2-3. Press.
Label 2 pieces B and 8 pieces D.

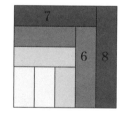

Blocks A & C
Make 2 of A (Lt Brown/Dk Green)
Make 8 of C (Dark Green/Red)

Blocks B & D
Make 2 of B (Lt Brown/Dk Green)
Make 8 of D (Dark Green/Red)

**BLOCK ASSEMBLY:**
**Complete Blocks A & C:** Make 10.
Sew #6 to the left side of #1-2-3-4-5.
Sew #7 to the top of #1-2-3-4-5-6.
Sew #8 to the left side of #1-2-3-4-5-6-7.

**Complete Blocks B & D:** Make 10.
Sew #6 to the right side of #1-2-3-4-5.
Sew #7 to the top of #1-2-3-4-5-6.
Sew #8 to the right side of #1-2-3-4-5-6-7.
NOTE: Use 4 Lt Brown/Dk Green Blocks for the corners.
Use 16 Dark Green/Red Blocks for sides, top and bottom.

Block E
Centers for Sides
Make 2

CENTERS FOR SIDES:
**Block E:**
Sew #1 to #2. Press.
Sew #3 to the top.
Sew #4 to the bottom of #1-2-3. Press.
Sew #5 to the left side of #1-2-3-4. Press.
Sew #6 to the top. Sew #7 to the bottom. Press.
Sew #8 to the left side. Press.
Make 2.

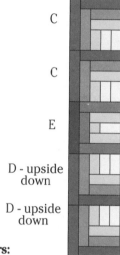

C

C

E

D - upside
down

D - upside
down

**Log Cabin Borders:**
**Side Columns:**
Sew blocks in a column:
C-C-E-D upside down-D upside down. Press.
Make 2.

**Left Side:**
Sew one column to the left side of the quilt. Press.

**Right Side:**
Turn the second column upside down. Sew this
column to the right side of the quilt. Press.

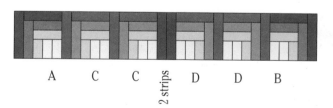

A | C | C | 2 strips | D | D | B

**Top and Bottom Borders:**
Sew blocks in a row:
A-C-C-2 Dark Brown strips-D-D-B. Press.
Make 2.
**Top:**
Sew one row to the top of the quilt. Press.
**Bottom:**
Turn the second row upside down.
Sew this row to the bottom. Press.

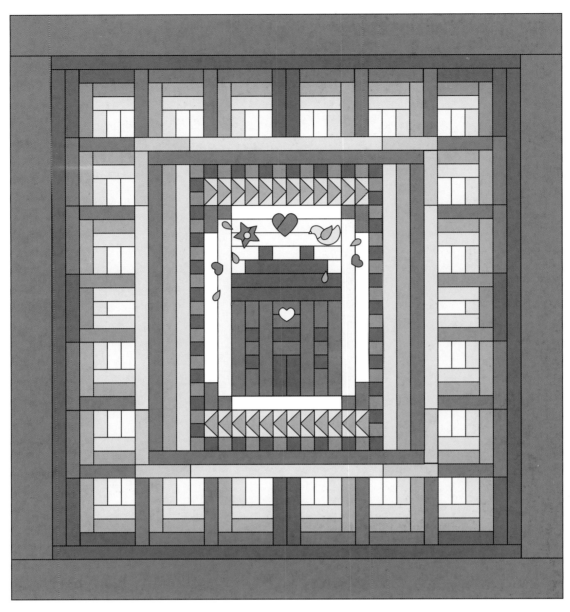

Birchwood House - Quilt Assembly

OUTSIDE BORDERS:

**Dark Brown Border #1:**
Cut strips 2½" wide by the width of fabric.
Sew together end to end.
Cut 2 strips 2½" x 70½" for sides.
Cut 2 strips 2½" x 68½" for top and bottom.
Sew side borders to the quilt. Press.
Sew top and bottom borders to the quilt. Press.

**Red Outer Border #2:**
Cut strips 6½" wide parallel to the selvage to prevent piecing.
Cut 2 strips 6½" x 74½" for sides.
Cut 2 strips 6½" x 80½" for top and bottom.
Sew side borders to the quilt. Press.
Sew top and bottom borders to the quilt. Press.

FINISHING:

**Quilting**:
See Basic Instructions on pages 24 - 26.

**Binding**:
Cut strips 2½" wide.
Sew together end to end to equal 346".
See Binding Instructions on page 26.

Birchwood Lane
Small House Quilt
see instructions
on page 38

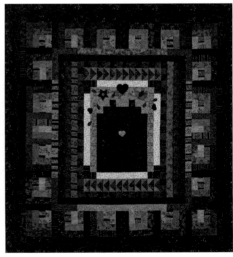

Birchwood Lane - Large House Quilt
large photos are on pages 50 - 51

# Smores Snowmen and Houses

pieced by Kayleen Allen
quilted by Julie Lawson

After a day building snowmen, we're snacking on smores inside
these cozy houses. You can almost smell the smoke rising from the
fire places, hear the crackling of roasting marshmallows, and don't
forget the chocolate!

Who can resist these cheery colors and graham cracker doors?

instructions on pages 13 - 15

Smores
'Jelly Roll'

Vibrant tulips bloom all year in a quilt that is as fresh as a Spring rain. Use speed piecing methods and watch your garden grow!

These fabulous flowers were designed in versatile blocks so you can easily alter the setting and change the number of blocks for an exciting look that is all your own.

instructions on pages 35 - 37

# Fresh Squeezed Tulips

*pieced by Kayleen Allen*
*quilted by Julie Lawson*

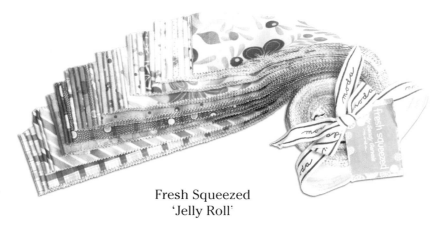

Fresh Squeezed
'Jelly Roll'

*The men in your family are going to love this quilt! Bring a touch of sophisticated style and old-world elegance to any room with this exquisite checkerboard design. Opulent natural tones take one back to the plush decor found in Victorian dens and libraries where gentlemen engaged one another at the chessboard while ladies sipped tea in the adjoining parlor.*

instructions on pages 27 - 30

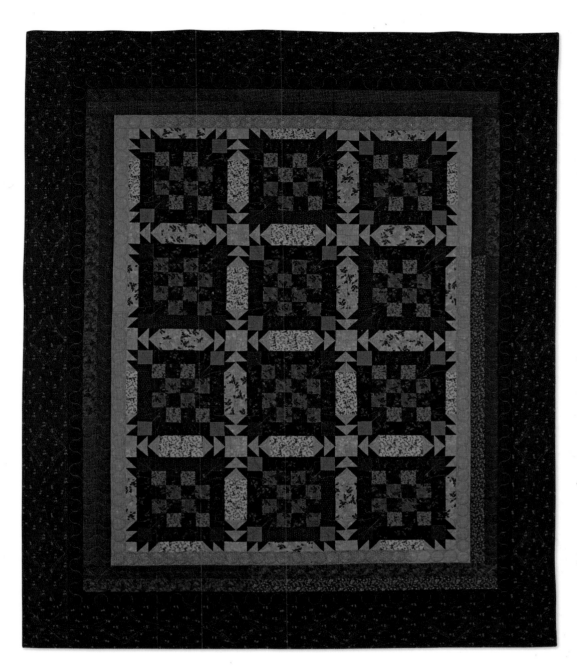

# Cranberry Wishes Checkerboard
### pieced by Lanelle Herron
### quilted by Julie Lawson

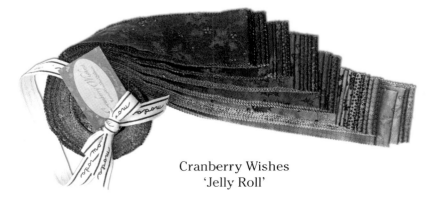

Cranberry Wishes
'Jelly Roll'

*Even if you can't afford a log cabin nestled in a forest, you can find your way there while dreaming beneath this snuggle-soft quilt. Bedecked in rich burgundy, forest green, and sandstone colors, this masterpiece is destined to become a family heirloom.*

instructions on pages 38 - 43